MW01165478

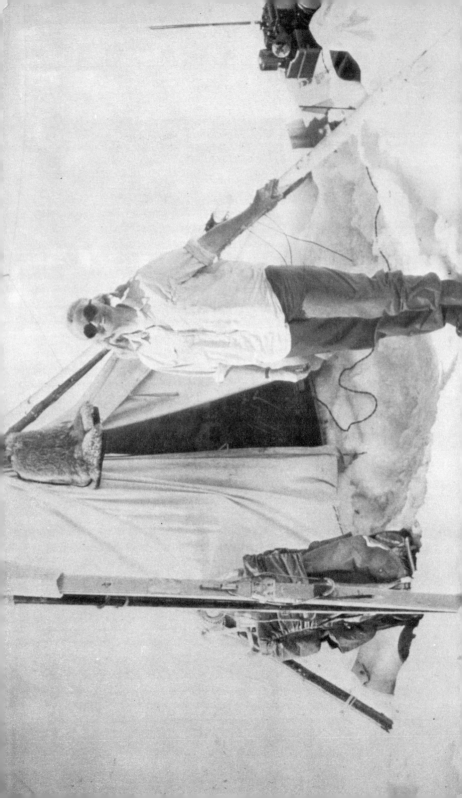

Denali Diary

Letters from McKinley

by Frances

(Opposite page)
Frances, in 1983
at Kahiltna base
camp.

Climbing party prepares for ascent from Base Camp.

Denali Diary

Letters from McKinley

by Frances Saunders Randall
(1924-1984)

CLOUDCAP • SEATTLE

Dedication

This book is dedicated to mountain climbers the world over, and to the brave pilots who rescue them.

I wish to acknowledge the help and encouragement of Al Randall, Claude Glenn, Cliff Hudson, Lowell Thomas Jr., Joan Weiss, Donna DeShazo and especially Frances' father, Nile Saunders, and her brother, David.

The Bavarians, 1977.

Contents

Lowell Thomas, Jr.

"Guardian Angel of McKinley"

"One Nine Victor, this is Kahiltna Base. Good morning! Landing conditions are . . . " It always perked me up to hear Frances Randall's cheery voice in my earphones after buzzing through One Shot Pass and while flying on up McKinley's Kahiltna Glacier to our 7000-foot high base camp. No sooner would I bring my plane to a stop than Fran would be right there to meet a new batch of climbers and help unload their gear, even though the temperature might be on the minus side of zero.

Indeed, Frances was, and still is the guardian angel of those who set foot on McKinley, and of those of us who do the flying. During the five seasons that I worked with her, I developed great admiration and a deep respect for this lady, who, herself, had climbed North America's highest peak. Her untimely death to cancer greatly saddened all who knew her and left a yawning gap that may never be filled.

Frances was personally concerned for the safety and welfare of every climber. Before they'd leave base camp she'd warn them of the various hazards, such as hidden crevasses on the lower glacier and, from her years of mountaineering experience, would offer suggestions regarding equipment and food and how to minimize the chances of coming down with high altitude sickness. Once they were on the mountain she would keep track of their progress via CB radio, sharing in their enthusiasm and relaying their messages to the outside world.

Kahiltna Base can become something of a Tower of Babel at the peak of the season, with climbers from many foreign lands as well as the US: Japan, Germany, France, Italy, Korea, Mexico, the USSR among others. As camp manager, Frances had to communicate with all of them, sometimes mediating disputes over tent sites, and especially over flying-out priorities once they were back down. All that, she handled superbly, having a good command of four or five languages and, just as important, a diplomatic skill that could have been useful even at the UN! Those qualities also were important in coordinating the inevitable rescues of injured or ill climbers—Frances relaying radio messages between the party in question and the plane or helicopter involved. Some of the most interesting writings in this book are her accounts of high altitude rescues.

Frances Randall was a warm, lively person who liked people; in return, they all liked her. And her love of McKinley was infectious. In a letter home she wrote:

"Few in this entire world have a home like mine, with Mt. McKinley out of my back window, Mt. Hunter (14000 feet) rising 7000 feet above the glacier about one half mile away, and Mt. Foraker, five-eighths of a mile away, rising 12000 feet above the glacier to 17000 feet. As I write, I'm listening to Mozart's 'Symphonia Concertante' and an occasional avalanche. The night is beautiful with the clouds blowing around Foraker and the Foraker-Crosson Traverse."

Though she's gone from this world, Frances' spirit lingers on, looking down upon those who climb and fly McKinley and its neighboring peaks — our Guardian Angel.

Lowell Thomas, Jr.
August 1, 1986

Frances, with the barnstorming Arctic Chamber Orchestra, on Aleutian Islands, 1977.

Mt. Frances, named in honor of the late author. Avalanche at center raises huge ice cloud.

Introduction

This book is made up of the letters that Frances wrote home from the Kahiltna Glacier Base Camp on Mt. McKinley during the summers of 1976 through 1983. These are personal letters to us, her father, her brother David and myself, her mother. But they are also the record of her activities, her diary perhaps, on the glacier. She first went to the glacier in 1975 for four days on her July 4th vacation from her job at Tundra Biome, University of Alaska, Fairbanks. One reason that Cliff Hudson asked her to take the job probably was because he knew a little of her past experience as a climber. She had begun climbing while she was working at Boeing in Seattle as a computer programmer and was a member of the Seattle Mountaineers. Eventually she met Al Randall, a supervisor in the tooling division at Boeing. After they were married, life became one round of mountain climbs. They bought a home between Issaquah and Bellevue, across Lake Sammamish and Lake Washington east of Seattle.

They climbed Mt. Rainier many times, of course, as well as Mt. Baker, Mt. St. Helens, Glacier Peak, Mt. Stuart, Mt. Adams, Mt. Olympus (twice), Mt. Index and many lesser peaks in the state of Washington. In Oregon, they climbed Mt. Jefferson and Mt. Hood, and in Canada, Mt. Garibaldi and Mt. Robson.

Then there was the joint expedition with the Japanese in 1967 to climb Mt. Bona (16420 feet) in the Wrangell Mountains near the Yukon border. The Japanese climbers were from Kobe, Japan, a sister city of Seattle. It was there that Frances became acquainted with Mr. Miyazaki, deputy mayor of Kobe City, who was her host when she went to Japan three years later. It was on that climb that Frances called us on the phone by radio from an ice cave.

In 1964 they climbed Mt. McKinley. They flew from Seattle, seventeen men and three women, on June 13, landed in Anchorage, Alaska, and took the train from there to the McKinley Park Headquarters. Then they walked across the tundra, forded two rivers and started up the Muldrow Glacier. Cliff Hudson dropped supplies for them at McGonagall Pass, coming in between storms. They established camps at intervals to rest and become acclimatized before climbing on. Karsten's Ridge was one of the most difficult portions of their route. Their last camp was at 17800 feet. On July 9, all but three reached the summit, the largest group ever to reach the top at that time. The three who did not go to the top were victims of altitude sickness. By July 16 they were all back down; they forded two rivers, the McKinley and Susitna, walked several miles to the highway, were picked up by a truck and were taken to Park Headquarters. They took the train to Fairbanks and flew back to Seattle.

One very interesting thing about this climb was that it represented the first communication with the world below from the summit. They made several telephone calls to relatives and friends, using a small battery-operated transmitter that was picked up by regular stations in Anchorage and Fairbanks. Frances fell in love with Mt. McKinley then and loved it all the rest of her life. She was convinced that the Mountain should have been given the Indian name, Denali, instead of the name of a President back in Washington, D.C.

In Mexico, their old friends, Norm Benton and Hans Zogg climbed with them Orizaba, Popocatepetl, Ixtaccihuatl and Colima. Pictures were taken down in the dormant crater of Popo (the Mexicans very sensibly gave this volcano a shorter name). Ixtaccihuatl is called the Sleeping Lady. They made friends with many Mexican climbers, including Consuelo Herrera. Almost every year after that, Frances visited Consuelo for a couple of weeks after Christmas and took side trips to the Mayan ruins in Yucatan and Guatemala.

Frances climbed Fujiyama as a result of a trip she made to Japan during the Exposition in 1970. Four people from Seattle had been invited to visit Kobe. It turned out that the other three could not go, so Frances went alone. She was the guest of the deputy mayor of Kobe and stayed in their guest house. She was accompanied most everywhere by a young lady who spoke English quite fluently. Some of the climbers, whom she had met on the American-Japanese Joint Expedition (AJJEX) in Alaska, took her to climb Fujiyama. The Japanese surely must be among the world's most courteous and entertaining of hosts as Frances was taken to so many interesting places, including the Kabuki Theater.

A Scandinavian princess was visiting Japan at that time, also to attend the Exposition. She was expected to attend a performance of the Kabuki Theater on the same evening that

Frances went. Princess Margarita (or whatever her name was) was a tall blond. When Frances, also a tall blond, walked in with the Japanese gentleman who was escorting her, all the audience rose to their feet thinking it was the princess. When they discovered that it was just a common American, they sat down. The Japanese man said, "Never mind Frances, you are my princess anyway." When Frances went to a beauty parlor to have her hair rearranged or fixed up (at that time she was wearing her hair in a beautiful mass of puffs all over her head), the lady owner of the shop called all her helpers over to see how Frances' hair was done.

Here is a letter from Claude Glenn, Frances' long time friend:

"Since I have always climbed, hiked and skied primarily for the pleasure of it, I have never kept any record of dates and times. Therefore, I can only generalize on my times with Frances.

"I first met Frances in March 1964, before she and Al went to McKinley. During the next eighteen years, Frances and I made numerous climbs on Mt. Rainier, Mt. Adams, Mt. St. Helens, Mt. Hood, Glacier Peak and Mt. Baker. We never climbed Mt. Olympus together. As you already know, Frances and I were running partners for years, this before running was popular as it is now. There was one training trip we particularly enjoyed—that was a run up Mt. Si in the morning and McClellan's Butte in the afternoon. Frances and I shared the responsibility of leading Mountaineer climbs and field trips. Frances was a worthy and reliable partner on these trips. Frances and I were rope partners on the 1967 AJJEX Expedition.

"It would be boring to you if I tried to recall all the fun hikes and climbs I enjoyed with Frances. The last long trip I made with Frances was the summer of 1981, on our hike from just north of the Columbia River at Stevenson, to White Pass, Washington."

It is evident from Frances' letters that she was glad to leave the Kahiltna Glacier each year, the equivalent of cabin fever probably. But the next spring she could hardly wait for the time to go again. She took hundreds of pictures on the glacier and I am truly sorry that we can't include them all in the book. I have read these letters several times now in the process of copying them, and one thing stands out above all others: the willingness of mountain climbers to cancel their own plans, schedules and wishes to go immediately to the rescue of another climber in trouble.

The following was written by Carol Howisey Carnahan, who was a member of the 1964 McKinley climbing group along with Frances and eighteen others.

"Frances was my friend for twenty years. Being with her was always an adventure whether we were backpacking or talking all night around my kitchen table. She was curious about everything: mountains, mathematics, linguistics, history, the stars, N,W. Indian culture, Mexican archaeology, wild flowers, music, animals and people of all sorts. She spoke Russian, a little Japanese, Athabascan Indian and fluent Spanish. Frances was an intellectual who turned her back on the Ivory Castle and embraced the whole world.

"I shared a tent with Frances on Mt. McKinley. Even being pinned down by a four-day blizzard didn't faze her. While the rest of us cowered in our sleeping bags, Frances crawled through the storm to the other tents and went visiting! Gregarious, funny and imaginative, she later got to know people from all over the world who came to the Kahiltna Glacier. Soon she came to be known as 'The Queen of the Kahiltna.' Although Frances grew up in an era when being female imposed many constraints, she knew no such boundaries.

"Frances co-organized the first large expedition to Mt. McKinley. It set many records. She then went on to climb five of the six highest mountains on the North American continent. With the help of friends, she built her own log cabin near Fairbanks and lived there without running water and other amenities for fifteen years. Frances was a violinist for the Fairbanks Chamber Orchestra. They toured Eskimo and Indian villages all over Alaska and slept on the gymnasium floor when the performance was over!

"After retiring from computing, Frances combined two most unlikely ways of making a living. She taught violin to children during the winter and managed the McKinley pilots' base camp on the Kahiltna Glacier every summer.

"When she died at age fifty-nine, Frances had nearly completed her second degree. Her first was in math; the second was in languages.

"In these ways and others Frances was a pioneer. While younger women are now beginning to venture out onto this kind of new ground, Frances and a very few others of her generation established the route. This is part of her legacy; her violin students are another.

"Frances never lost her fighting spirit even during the last months of her life. Like a true mountaineer she was brave to the end. I miss her very much. A part of her will always be with me."

Cliff Hudson employed Frances to manage the base camp from the first year on and she invariably turned to him for help in time of trouble. He wrote us the following:

"Frances was a very nice person with a heart of gold, always trying to help someone out. Everyone that knew her sure does miss her. But that is life. We are all here for a short time, it seems. And Frances left fond memories in many hearts."

Several other pilots flew climbers in and out of the base camp, but one of the most frequent was Lowell Thomas, Jr.

Very often he helped with the rescues and many times brought people who wished to interview Frances.

Climbers in camp often asked Frances to play her violin and took pictures of her playing. They seemed to consider it an oddity, but it really was an important part of her life. She began the study of piano when she was six and changed to violin when she was eleven. She loved the violin and played in the orchestra both in high school and at the University of Washington. The violin teacher there at that time was a former pupil of the noted Leopold Auer. Because of the War (World War II) the University orchestra was asked to play with the Seattle Symphony, since so many players had gone off to the Army. That is how Frances happened to have the opportunity to play under the baton of Sir Thomas Beecham. He always reminded Frances of Dr. Watson of the Sherlock Holmes series on the radio at that time. While working at Boeing, she studied with Francis Armstrong for five years.

In 1970 taking her dog, her cat, her violin and the key to Roscoe and Carol Carnahan's cabin, she went to College, Alaska, leaving behind her in Seattle the unhappiness of her divorce from Al Randall. In a few months she bought a lot and built her first cache, in which she lived while building a cabin, with a good bit of financial help from her father.

Frances got a job as a computer programmer and joined the University of Fairbanks Symphony. She soon had several pupils, too. She herself was a pupil of Paul Rosenthal, former pupil of Heifitz, and this was one of the most pleasant experiences of Frances' life. For fourteen years, Frances toured with the Arctic Chamber Orchestra every fall to a different section of the state. In one of the old Russian towns she went into a church and somehow became locked in and couldn't get out. It was about time for the plane to leave when she finally managed to climb up to one of the windows and open it. She hailed a man passing by in the street and he came and opened the door for her.

Twice a year, Frances played in the orchestra for the Fairbanks Light Opera Theater. She also played in a trio: violin, viola and cello. During the latter part of the summer while home on vacation, she studied with Camilla Wicks, distinguished concert artist, now professor of violin at the University of Michigan.

The following was written by Lesley Salisbury, Frances' longtime Alaskan friend:

"I remember the first time I saw Frances. It was in September. I believe it was her first year at the University of Alaska. We'd gone to the Patty Gym to see hikers and the runners come in at the end of the marathon. Our boys were hiking it, and our friend, Pat Pine, came in just ahead of Fran. We saw her cooling down after that rough twenty six miles. We were struck by the tall stranger who was right up there near the first. When our younger boy came in, we had to lift him into the van. He was too stiff, he couldn't lift his legs to climb in. We didn't know Fran's name, but we talked about her at dinner that evening. The next year, the boys had learned enough from her to know both how to warm up and cool down after the race.

"The next week, Tuesday rolled around and it was symphony and there she was again! How could one miss that blond coif sailing along, six feet up there? And she was carrying a violin case!

"I'm not sure if we were stand partners that first season, but we were often, for many years to come. We were on chamber music tours nearly always. As we got to know one another, new and interesting things were discovered about Frances. She was a real mountain climber. She knew several languages. She was bright. She was interested in math and computers.

"I asked her to take on our youngest, Druska, as a violin pupil. Fran was steadfastly patient and understanding and was a good model. Soon Druska began to play nicely. In the difficult years, those teen times, Fran was so good to both Druska and me, too. We began a pattern which we maintained until Fran could no longer come to orchestra. She would come for Druska's lesson on Tuesday after school and then the two of us would go to symphony after having dinner with the family. At first, all four children were there. Gradually each child left for schools outside Alaska and the last two or three years, there were just the three of us; Lee, Fran and I. Often we'd play duets for fun if there was no orchestra meeting.

"When the boys were in junior high, Fran would take them and a friend or two and take them rock climbing. She taught the rudiments, always emphasizing safety and the value of planning. It was interesting to hear them talking about her: 'Fran is strict,' they'd say, 'but we know she tells us what's important.' That's respect! Later, when Lex had trouble with algebra, Fran tutored him. She seemed more and more part of the family. She continued to come for supper up until when I had to take her to the hospital for the last time.

"I really can't close without honoring the lessons she taught me. We shared a lot of jokes, a lot of grief, a lot of experience over the years. On several Arctic Chamber tours we had some nervous experiences. Flying in South Eastern, for example. I don't like to fly if I have to look up at mountains in the fog. Once we flew out of Nome for hours, looking for St. Lawrence Island, with no radio contact and a pilot who was new to Alaska. We were flying over the Chukchi Sea under low clouds. Everyone was airsick, but one of the guys, Fran and me (presumably the pilot, too). I figured we had to be in Siberia by now. Fran and I began to talk and plan what to do if anything happened. She read each person's needs so clearly: who would be likely hysterical, who we could depend on to carry out a specific job, etc. How to take sensible precautions. After that I always kind of gravitated toward her when there was any sense of emergency. We often sat together on trips, but we were not room mates, since Fran did not need the long hours of sleep that I need.

"Until the last day, when she left for New York City and I for Australia, we were good friends, I am proud to say. Easy together, perfectly steady and sure, always free to do as we wished and to be who we were.

"Now that I have cancer, I'm grateful for her example, her grit. She's a good example. I think of her often, still feel close to her, dream of her. Not every friend knows how to live and how to die. Fran did!"

Frances did not feel well during the fall of 1983, and in January 1984 the doctors in Fairbanks discovered that she had cancer. She came home and commuted back and forth to Seattle for treatments. On April 14 she drove high up Derby Canyon and picked a bouquet of wild flowers for me; she had been bringing me wild flowers since she was a little girl. On April 15 she took her new black and white collie pup and went back to Seattle to attend a concert by Camilla Wicks. Carol Carnahan and Atsuko Ohtaka went to the concert with her.

On April 16 she and the pup flew back to Alaska. Frances called on April 21; she was back in the hospital being fed intravenously. The doctors there warned Frances that her cancer might "explode" at any time and that would be the end. Our nephew, Dr. Robert Saunders of Washington, D.C., came to accompany Frances and they left for New York City, via Seattle and Sloan-Kettering, arriving there on May 1. Rob called us at 9:30 the next morning to tell us that Frances had died a few minutes before. She was brought back here for cremation. Her father took her ashes to Fairbanks.

Frances' mountain climbing friends in Seattle held a memorial service at the home of Bill Zauche. Mrs. Sagan, Frances' old Russian teacher and friend, said a prayer. Al Randall showed some slides of some of the many trips that Frances had participated in over the years. All those present signed a card which Al Randall brought to us.

In Fairbanks, Professor Gordon Wright, conductor of the symphony, and Jane Aspness, manager, arranged a beautiful memorial service. It opened with the musicians playing the "Andante (Air for the G String)" and "Gavotte from a Bach Suite." Then Professor Wright spoke briefly about Frances' long association with the symphony and the Arctic Chamber Orchestra. This was followed by a string quartette playing a Brahms andante. Then the Reverend Jean Dementi, Episcopal minister, told of her conversation with Frances a few days before and said a prayer.

The musical portion closed with a brass sextet playing the Gounod composition that they had played only a few days before for Pope John Paul II and President Reagan when they were in Fairbanks. Chief Ranger Robert Gerhard of the Denali Park Service told of Frances' long cooperation with them during rescue missions and other Park affairs. When he had finished his talk, Frances' father, Nile Saunders, delivered Frances' ashes to Mr. Gerhard. He took them to the glacier and delivered them to Cliff Hudson, pilot and long friend of Frances, who flew them to the top of a mountain, which Mr. Gerhard said would now be called Mt. Frances.

Leathie McCarthy Saunders,
Peshastin, Washington

June 21, 1980.   The young Catholic priests who were in camp were members of a climbing group, which also included a professional chef and a plumber. In her conversation with the group, Frances, being a musician, asked about the Gregorian chant, which she had heard of, but had not heard. They explained to her that all young men studying for the priesthood were required to learn the Gregorian chant, and then the three of them sang it for her in unison.

June 18, 1979.   Frances wrote: "A lady and baby are going part way up. (The baby likes it.)" Nothing more was ever said about how far they went, or when they came back. I have always wondered. That baby by now would be six or seven years old and probably is climbing mountains on his own power.

Frances did not mention this in her letters, but she told us about it later on in the summer when she was here at home. One group of climbers from Southern Europe (it was not the Italians) tried to bribe their mountain guide to sign their certificate proving they had reached the summit when they did not. He refused.

Some of the names chosen by the climbing groups were quite fantastic, for instance, the *Colorado Cuties.* I am sure that this was not a "bunch of dumb blonds." They were serious and capable mountain climbers. I do not know how many of them made the top. Two of them climbed in spite of a strep throat and an infection. I do hope that Sarah got her skis back! *Fireworks* surely was a suitable name for the group that started out July 4th.

The author, in a quiet moment on the Mountain.

Author's pen and ink sketch. Mounts McKinley, Foraker and Hunter.

Chapter One — 1976

"I'm writing from the Kahiltna Glacier"

June 26: I'm writing from the Kahiltna Glacier. Beautiful flight in. The sun has set behind Foraker, so it's cold. I had dinner with two climbers from Oregon, who are really nice young college students. I brought the lettuce from home, and also the dill and onions. (You can tell George and Mary when you see them.) So we had a Washington salad. Bobby should be coming in next Wednesday if the weather is good. There are seventeen climbing parties on the Mountain, about one hundred fifty people. The radio should be coming back in a few days. My new tent is beautiful, and it is really a pleasure after all the years of not having any except a small one. My pen is cold. I haven't started my Japanese yet, as I've been working every minute since I got here. It's really getting cold.

Sgook surely has been giving me some peculiar looks the last few days. We arrived in Anchorage, and went to the Ranchero. Then we started driving and then stayed at a hotel. Next morning we jumped in the Cessna and took off. She rode on the floor behind the pilot. She did very well, but obviously didn't like the noise. This afternoon I saw her sitting on the glacier staring around at the mountains. Tonight in the tent she stared and stared at me tying down the tent opening. We had beautiful weather and flew over scattered clouds. Then there were several more flights, and now everyone is gone except me and a couple from Poland.

Last night a three-member American party from Anchorage came in. The first member was not talking to the other two members, and vice-versa, about who had carried the most weight uphill. Then eight Japanese came in, and then a nine-member Japanese team with three women. Later a two-man Italian party came in. I met the first one and he had frostbitten hands. I fed him and helped him get his parka on. Then he went over to see Sgook. Sgook was very popular with the Japanese and the Italians, particularly Toni with the frostbitten hands and

1

fingers. The weather has not been the greatest with only one flight today. Sgook sleeps in the tent with me and runs around on the glacier when I'm out walking, but otherwise is chained up. She still is in the center of activity.

June 28. Two parties came in yesterday, one from Australia and the other from various parts of the Lower Forty-eight. They left to climb immediately. A third fellow joined the party of two from Oregon and they left for Foraker. Two of them knew some of the people that I knew from the University of Alaska. In the meantime a party of thirteen returned from the Mountain—some of them are from the Mt. Rainier guide service, *Rainier Mountaineering, Inc. (RMI)*. Next, I got sick after supper, probably on some freeze-dried food or the water. The pollution problem is terrible on the Mountain. In the night, three climbers came in and are now waiting for four of their buddies who did a different route. They have climbed extensively and plan to do Squamish Chief and some rock around Leavenworth. The weather has been much better. I am worried about the three on Foraker as they are doing a bad route and everything is avalanching.

June 29. Around 4:00 a.m., the plane came in for the Italian team and, later, we learned that Toni might lose eight fingers. Later, a ten-member Japanese team arrived. Then the Polish team came back from ferrying a load up to 14000 feet; they were met by Carl Tobin from Fairbanks, who is also a member of the Alaska Alpine Club, as I am. Late in the evening another man came in looking for a climbing party that was already on the Mountain. After two weeks, it was unlikely that he could find his team, so he finally joined a two-man team from San Francisco. One of the men had been a mathematics professor for the University of California at Berkeley, I believe, and the other was a physics professor at the University of California. Then an old man came in with a small backpack and no sleeping bag to climb McKinley by himself. Everyone tried to talk him out of going. Ray Genet found him the next morning, sleeping on the ice, and persuaded him to come back. A five-man team of Genet's came in this afternoon with a man from Portland, Oregon, who had minor frostbite. All those that were leaving got out, except for eight members of a ten-member Japanese team from Osaka, the sister city of Spokane, Washington. Everyone got out. The weather looks peculiar. One more from the *RMI* group is coming in tomorrow if the weather is satisfactory.

I practiced my violin today out on the glacier. It is not the most ideal way to practice, but it is better than nothing. Meanwhile Sgook slept in my tent. Sgook watches the planes take off and land and seems to be aware that this is an important part of the glacier. No one in Base Camp tonight except Sgook and me. Jim, the student from Oregon State, went down to Talkeetna today to complete his survey on McKinley for his senior project in physical education. Yesterday and today were really tedious with the old man, people coming in demanding to go out, and temperamental weather.

The other four Englishmen came down. Cliff and Doug flew out the thirteen Washington people (their doctor was from Colorado). Also the three guys from Colorado went out. I had met them last year and they were nice. Then the eight Englishmen went out. They were OK too. There was a girl in the party of Washington climbers. She came over and talked to me last night and was quite nice. One of their party had to be flown out earlier because of pulmonary edema. About six Japanese just came in to climb, but I haven't talked to them yet. It is raining now and it should be snowing in a little while. I guess the temperature has been very hot in Talkeetna. I surely am wondering about *Viking I.* The Colorado climbers are going to send me a newspaper.

June 30. 11:30 p.m. Avalanches everywhere. Six of the Japanese took a load out and returned. Four Colorado climbers came back after twenty-some days on a difficult route. Doug, who works for Cliff, brought the battery in last night, and today I reset the radio tent. Because of differences in melting rates of unexposed and exposed snow surfaces, it is frequently necessary to reset tents when temperatures are high. I've been reading and studying some. Bobbie isn't here yet. Two ravens came by again today.

July 3. The weather has been socked in for days now, and no plane has come in except for a chopper that came into the pass, but no one could see it. The six Japanese climbers relayed more equipment up the Mountain today and came back. I had supper and tea with them: rice and seaweed. They gave me a school flag. Between Japanese, Spanish, Italian and English we managed to converse. We had interesting talks about Japan, the Mountain, Mexico, themselves and me. I told them about

3

the Ohtakes and they may see them in Fairbanks. By that time I should be in Washington. As it is impossible to fly in, Bobbie, of course, is not here and neither is the radio, which I'm sure is fixed by this time. The four Colorado climbers are still here, obviously awaiting anxiously the return of good weather. All of these climbers are nice. I'm worried about the three climbers on Foraker as that is the area where the chopper turned around. Those were very nice young men, so I hope they are OK. They didn't plan on bad weather, which they should have, but they did take a lot of equipment that they talked about caching at a lower altitude. The amount of new and wet snow that we have had would not have been good for the route they chose to climb, which was a rib and then a long traverse. Tomorrow only the four Colorado climbers and myself will be left at Base Camp unless the other Colorado team comes in.

I'm reading, studying, talking, resting and exercising. Also resetting my tent and rearranging it continually. I wish I had Smoke here. I'm now reading *Zen and the Art of Motorcycle Maintenance.* This book was handed down to the Oregon climbers from one of the Englishmen, who was a philosopher (the Colorado dentist told me this). The Colorado team gave me *One Day in the Life of Ivan Denisovich,* and I gave them *The Susitna Valley Chronicle,* the *Menagerie Manor* and *Pyramid Power.*

This is the end of Frances' letters from the Mountain in 1976. (Theodore Roosevelt took *Alice in Wonderland* on a hunting safari to Africa, so let's not criticize the mountain climbers for their choice of literature.)

Chapter Two — 1977

"The poor man
may lose eight fingers"

June 24. I'm waiting at Anchorage for takeoff to Fairbanks, so I can teach all day. The plane encountered a little turbulence after we passed McKinley, which was spectacular. We are on our way down toward Tanana Flats. I look forward to teaching for about ten hours and I do hope the VW works. I'll be calling in the next day or two. PS: I catch the 3:10 plane back to Anchorage tomorrow and then drive to Talkeetna.

June 25. Saturday morning. I'm in the beauty shop. Sgook is with me. Smoke and Kitty are OK.

In-flight to Anchorage! Mt. McKinley is to the right with our route up the Harper Glacier directly in front. Foraker comes into view, and that is where I go—between McKinley and Foraker on the Kahiltna. Later, I drove to Talkeetna.

July 1. Part of the *RMI* group came in today. Later, the wind velocity picked up. There was a lot of turbulence on the Kahiltna below the landing strip, and there were cross winds on the landing field. The landing strip is in a relatively protected area but the winds have gotten stronger. Higher on the Mountain the wind velocity must be extremely high.

The Genet party of five hasn't come in yet. Hopefully they are OK, along with over a hundred others at various places on the Mountain.

July 2. It stormed. Finally, part of the German party showed up, but still no Genet party. At every radio contact, Genet wants to know if his party is in. Doug brought in Charlie Porter, who does a lot of solo climbing. Charlie lives in Maine.

July 3. The weather stormed out. Cliff flew in a couple of times. Mike and Cliff took out the Genet party, which was led by Cricket. Genet has two girl guide/cooks that I know of and have met. The rest of the German party arrived. The Japanese party, led by the famous Japanese guide, whom I had met last year, flew out with Cliff. They gave me a present at 7:30 a.m. when I knocked on their tent to find out if they had flown in with Cliff, how many there were, and if they had seen the Genet party. They had seen the Genet party at Windy Corner, which is around 12000 feet to 14000 feet. All the Genet party is out; one of the party had another case of frostbitten fingers. Charlie Porter is ready with his buddy, Beaucaire, to do a risky route on Mt. Hunter.

July 4. Late last night a Japanese team of five, including one lady, came in. They are from the island south of the largest island and their town, Kitakyushushi, is the northern seaport on this island. They manufacture pipe and made a lot of the Alyeska pipe. Later, two park rangers brought down a German who was with the Swedish team. He has pulmonary edema. Doug just got in to fly him out in the morning. Weather is bad in Talkeetna. There is about a 10000-foot ceiling with some fog. Overhead is about five to fifteen percent blue sky. Wind is calm to 5 mph. This is a very quiet July 4th so far.

July 5. Another five-member Japanese team came in today. It snowed about a foot last night. Sgook and I went out and walked straight down the runway and diagonalled back and forth coming back so the pilots could tell where the snow is. Without shadows it is very hard to judge where the snow surface is. Then the weather was bad in Talkeetna and bad again here. Now there are twelve to fly out. Charlie Porter and Gary Beaucaire are going to do an awful route on Hunter. Now that it has snowed so much, they should be waiting for the mountain to avalanche out. The four-man German party, including two Americans, that walked up the Kahiltna are about ready to leave to climb the West Buttress. One of the Germans has tendencies toward pulmonary edema, so we'll see what happens. Sgook is the friendliest little dog, and the Japanese, in general, seem to be the nicest to her, except for the one Italian who had frostbite. He was so happy to see a friendly little dog. The poor man may lose eight fingers. I have received no letters so far, but I've heard it may take four days for letters to come from Anchorage to Talkeetna.

On July 10, Frances called from College. She was there for a few days to teach and do some work for Tundra Biome. She rode from Talkeetna on the train. She would go back on Tuesday or Wesnesday for two more weeks on the Mountain.

July 18. I just received your letter, but haven't read it. I'm fine and I must get this out as there may not be a plane for

6

awhile. I just got through working the runway over and I miss Sgook. Yesterday a TV crew was here and interviewed me. I'll be alone on the glacier now. The Polish-American scientific crew is up the glacier about two miles; I talk to them once a day and, with luck, to Talkeetna four times a day. There is one team left on the Mountain. I guess, with everyone gone, I should be able to get some work and practicing done. Say "Hello" to Lilly, Spot and Molly, also Georgette.

The last note I wrote in a great hurry while lying on my stomach in my tent on the snow so I could get it out on the plane. Aunt Mary wrote a nice letter along with yours. Everyone is gone now and I'm alone for at least four to six days, I think. I was happily reading *Chariot of the Gods* and about the Sumerians when the storm hit, so I had to go out and restake everything down. It's snowing now and very windy. Tomorrow I can make ice cream.

In another hour I have to try to contact the Polish-American scientific team, and then Talkeetna. There are six climbers on the Mountain who left this morning and are part of the TV crew. Charlie Porter and Rick are on Crosson. *RMI* finally got out before the weather deteriorated and they left me an incredible number of candy bars and Wyler's Lemonade, plus some freeze-dried foods and paper towels. After getting to know them, I thought they were an interesting group and they had a good climb. They knew some of the people I did, including Staley and Charlie, and one of the guides had heard of Rev. Sprague. Incidentally, where is he going?

Also, if it is not too much trouble, could you find out the name of the man who is the violin teacher at the University of Washington? Now that no one is here, I have time to read, practice and think, plus work on the runway.

July 19.   After spending one day alone, I was joined by two climbers who came back from McKinley and Cliff flew in four German climbers to do Foraker; now somebody high up in the Park is coming in. I was getting a lot of reading done, but the Germans will soon move out. They know Carl and Anne. Cliff just brought your letter, which I haven't read yet. It snowed last night and it has been pretty good today. One of the Germans and I worked on the airstrip. My German is getting better. What a jumble of languages! Tonight I will try to talk to the Polish-American team again.

July 25. I'm still on the glacier. Four Germans are on Foraker. I watch Foraker at 8:00 a.m., 12:00 noon, 4:00 p.m. and 8:00 p.m. for signals in case there is trouble. Foraker is a very difficult mountain. Last night four came in who had done the Muldrow and skied down the West Buttress. One of them was Sylvester, who has done some parachute jumping in Hollywood for the James Bond series. Sylvester is a mortal enemy of Charlie Porter, and vice versa by now, because, he said, Charlie had accused him of taking four candy bars on Baffin Island. It goes beyond that: one of the park rangers told Charlie something or other about Sylvester and by the time he was through Charlie Porter was ready to smear Sylvester all up and down the Kahiltna Glacier. Anyway Charlie and Rick had already left to ski down the Kahiltna. Hopefully, they will not meet in Talkeetna.

Then, in addition to all the news on the Kahiltna, the Polish-American team flew out today. After spending a couple of weeks and several miles up the glacier doing their thing for science, they were able to leave. This whole venture amounted to bringing the Polish scientists over here, plus two Americans, to study the deposits of polluting elements in the ice for the last fifty to two-hundred years. Before Charlie Porter left, I gave him a violin lesson on the Kahiltna and he was enchanted. Charlie is quite a character and an extremely noted climber. Here on the Kahiltna one runs into everybody and everything.

Mike Fisher who works for Jim Sharpe, who bought out Sheldon Flying Service in Talkeetna, was in today to take out Sylvester and crew. Mike was in Ireland last year and somewhere in his history (ancestry) the name McDermot exists. He says that with the magic password of a good Irish name you are in like Flynn in Ireland. I told him I was from the McCarthys and he seemed to be impressed. Bush pilots are curious creatures.

Well, I surely wish Sgook were here, but I'm sure the glare of the reflection from the glacier would be too much. I'm reading about Stonehenge now, and have a lot more to do.

Oh, yes! Four of the six Coloradoans are still on the Mountain. They don't seem to be doing much of anything, from what I hear. Then there is one more team that Mike is bringing in. It is not clear whether they are from Spain or Italy. Talkeetna does not seem to bother with such details. To make the most of all the Kahiltna activities, we had a National Park Service (NPS) VIP from Seattle-Bellevue here to inspect conditions on the glacier. He was accompanied by the local McKinley Park ranger. They made one trip to the Polish-American camp. The Park people "bumped" five Japanese who should have flown off sooner. The Japanese did an extremely difficult route on the Mountain and were very tired. The group included one woman. International relations have been strained at times among the Americans, Japanese, Germans and Italians.

July 26. I talked to Talkeetna this morning and apparently another Japanese group is coming into Talkeetna this noon from Anchorage. Most of the Japanese stay at Jack Kim's Anchorage Fur Factory and I guess he has had as many as sixty Japanese staying in his store coming or going to the Mountain, as tourists, or for other varied reasons to visit Alaska.

The weather last night was rainy and snowy and still is. Flying conditions are almost impossible, so the Japanese may have a wait in Talkeetna. Please pet Spot and Molly for me. Thanks for the birthday cards and California Poppy. Once in awhile I see an insect or some ravens.

It continues to rain and rain. I worked on the landing strip and got wet, so I'm trying to dry out in my tent. This series of events is nothing unusual. If the weather keeps on, the pilots are going to need pontoons instead of skis to land. The strip is a mess and I needed the exercise. Otherwise things are fine, but I surely miss Sgook and Kitty and Smoke. Fido by now is the equivalent of about one-hundred and forty years, which is really incredible.

I've been reading *Stonehenge Decoded,* which you gave me for a Christmas present. After this it's back to *Computo Azteca.* Intermixing all of this is Russian, Koyukon and that violin that I just hate to play. I wish there were some way to improve its tone. It's a beautiful violin, but the upper strings are terrible. *Stonehenge* is fascinating and the more I read of antiquities, the more fascinating I find this field. Now I wish I knew Gaelic, so I could read in the libraries of Ireland, and also I wish I could know more about the Welsh. Well, anyway, I have plenty to do.

July 27. It still continues to rain and rain and the landing strip is getting very waterlogged. I talked to Talkeetna a couple of times and it was decided to cancel all flights today. I worked on the landing strip and shoveled a lot of snow. By now I'm thoroughly convinced that shoveling snow must be one of my greatest contributions to the earth, since I've done so much of

9

it. Well, besides shoveling snow, I made a survival cook-and-food kit for Cliff's tent along with the radio.

If it stops raining for any length of time, I have to recharge the battery for the radio with the gasoline generator, and reset my tent. Exercise today consisted of working in the rain shoveling show, of course, and walking the landing strip to check for holes and resetting the black landing bags. There are four of these to give the pilots some sense of depth. Fortunately, I brought my "break-up" boots up here, so walking the soggy strip wasn't too bad.

I continue to watch Foraker, where the four Germans, are and hope they are OK. The avalanches were coming off Foraker and Hunter last night like fire and brimstone. You can't believe the immensity of these avalanches. The freezing level is about 500-1500 feet above where I am, but it still is not too cold. From the weather reports there are high winds from Big D (Denali) and out west. I listen to Bethel and was hearing Gambel and Savoonga on St. Lawrence, Holy Cross and other places. I hear both English and the Eskimo languages, but, unfortunately, the closest I have come to Athabaskan country is Holy Cross and St. Mary's, which I don't hear too often or too well.

I continue to read *Stonehenge* and am nearing the end of the book, but I must go back and start drawing out the Stonehenge Calendar. Recent discoveries by the author have definitely determined that it was used to predict, over centuries, the rising and setting of the sun and moon at their highest and lowest declination, the eclipses and the equinoxes. The motion of the moon is complicated because it has, as you recall, an 18.6-year cycle from its highest to lowest declination; this is why we see the moon some years very high in the sky, and other years not so high. Then, of course, it appears higher in our winter months.

I've become interested in the Hyperboreal people, the Sumerians, and wish I knew more of Pliny's writings. The Boreal people, according to Pliny, had one day and one night and lived up north. That would have to be true if they had the one-day/one-night phenomenon and it would have had to be close to the North Pole. This could only have been when conditions were quite different and the North was tropical. According to Pliny, they were visited by a god from Pleiades about every eighteen or twenty years, which was in accordance with the lunar cycle. Throughout ancient history, mythology and legends, Pleiades seems to have been very important.

I've written to Mary, Helen, Buddy, Frank and Jane, Roscoe and Carl, Gordon and various other people.

I hope Charlie Porter and Rich make it across those rivers down by Petersville, as they surely must be rising very high by now. They are quite a problem anyway, but with all of this rain they couldn't have picked a much worse time to go down the Kahiltna. And the Germans couldn't have picked a much worse time to be on Foraker. I watch for flares four times a day as their distress signal, but the clouds have been so thick at times, I don't think you could see an atomic explosion over there.

Hi to Lilly, Spot and Molly. Thanks again for the pressed poppy. I reread your letters when the plane doesn't come in and there is no mail.

July 28.   Today I reset my tent and the radio tent, which required a lot of shoveling snow. The weather cleared up last night and it was beautiful today. I also charged the battery for the radio. Doug brought the three Japanese from Nagasaki University, who will do the West Buttress.

I haven't been able to spot the Germans on Foraker though that may be their tracks at about 16500 feet. It's a long way away. If that was their tracks, they should be here in one to three days. The Colorado party should have moved back to 14000 feet today.

July 29.   Today Doug stopped by to pick up the Polish radio and batteries on his way to their camp to pick up more gear. This means he has made at least twelve trips for them.

Then I spent time shoveling snow and resorting food left by climbers, which is to go out. After that, I decided to survey that landing strip, including the length and the altitude gain. I had no level, so I made one out of a plastic bag, pencil and water, which I attached to my ice axe. I had no long measuring tape, so I used a long bamboo pole. As I needed to make only one such measurement, it wasn't bad. The alignments were made with three flags in a straight line and one at a right angle. These provide the reference points. I measured the bamboo pole with a long string. Stonehenge, I guess, inspired this venture in which I worked with things I had on hand. I used a flat square board to try to determine my right angles and also my sighting angles. It looked like this:

11

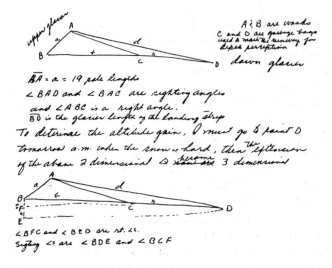

Since I had no ruler of any type to measure with, the closest information I had was scales from the maps. Neither map specified that any scaled distance specified another distance. The contour lines are from each 100 feet, but I have no reference. *Mountaineering: The Freedom of the Hills* gives scaling 1:25000 where one half inch is approximately one mile, and 1:62500 where one inch is approximately one mile. From this information, and the scales of 1:25000 and 1:50000 on my two maps, I could deduce the approximate distance, maybe. Otherwise, I could solve from the information I had that one degree at forty degrees latitude equals sixty-nine miles approximately, and calculate from the known mean radius of the earth, the distance of one degree to zero degrees latitude. Then, by differential calculus, I could determine the distance of one degree at sixty-three degrees fifty-seven minutes, which is the approximate latitude of our location. Washburn's maps give the scaled distance every five feet. Anyway, from one of these methods, I should be able to design my ruler. After that I can measure my string, which is the distance from B to A on the upper glacier.

I've noticed some interesting things about glacial flow and sink holes: it appears most glacial disturbances are natural, but many can be enhanced or caused by littering or just simply by traveling through an area. Glaciers have a tendency to melt where some foreign object is dropped. Their natural melt pattern is a misshapen paraboloid. As melt increases, the size, including depth and diameter, increases, which increases the natural size of this natural solar furnace.

Such a melt pattern should form perfect paraboloids at the North and South poles where the melt pattern would be equal from all directions during the twenty-four hour day when the sun rolls around the horizon. Here, at a lower latitude with some mountain shadow, the melt patterns are nearly perfect for most of the paraboloid; but as the Arctic night approaches and the sun sinks lower in the sky, it becomes less effective (intense) and there are fewer sunny hours.

Glacial flow is weird, because many tremendous forces are at work. There are surface disturbances, variable surface areas with basic convex and concave structures. The concave ones have tendencies to become paraboloids, but due to glacial flow, this is inhibited unless the flow is restricted for some reason, such as rock underneath or other glaciers. The melt underneath, which is river-like or maybe a river, causes further problems in the flow of the glacier. Anyway, you must be tired of all these long-winded discussions.

Finally, I was able to find the length of an inch. None of the maps were any help since all measures were proportional. Some maps, but not mine, actually use an inch length in their scaling. The best I came up with was one kilometer equals one minute on Brad Washburn's McKinley map, which still did not give the information. I finally arrived at the inch from the band around some envelopes I had purchased, which described the envelope size, and the envelope. Neither of the other methods were usable since scaling varies for maps, and for the second method I had only the mean radius of the earth and not the correct radius for this latitude. In the process of trying to find an inch, I discovered a simple method to divide lines or chords into an odd or even number of segments without measuring. If I could do this for odd angles in an arc, it would be great: it would solve the mystery of pi.

I still haven't seen the Germans. I will be happy to see them. I had hoped to come out with them. I had expected to come out earlier, but the climbing season has gone on and on. I'm alone about all the time now except for very short times when Doug comes in, which has been infrequent. The climbers, of course, are on the Mountain, and no one is waiting to fly out. Cliff has been in a couple of times, but not lately. He is doing a lot of the float plane and Piper Cub work. The float plane usually is used to take fishermen to the lakes and most of the Cub work is for the mining interests around here. On the radio I not only listen to all the weather data on the various small stations that check with Wien Airlines at Bethel, but also I frequently hear the miners. The Colorado climbers should be at 17000 feet today, and the Japanese should be at 10000 feet or 12000 feet.

I'll call as soon as I get out. Hello to Lilly and pet Spot and Molly.

July 31. The Germans arrived yesterday and it was really great to see them. As the first one arrived, just before 8:00 p.m., the fog settled in. I was playing "Watch on the Rhine," on my violin; I turned around and there they were, way out on the glacier. The weather was beautiful then. They were about three hours away and moving fast. They had brought lots of food, but they had had to bivouac in an ice cave for three days with emergency rations at a very high altitude. When the storm was over, they climbed to the top and came back to where most of their food was on the Mountain. Yesterday, I thought I had seen something strange about eight to ten miles away, but could not tell for sure. I had given up hope as Cliff had spotted them low on the Mountain and thought they were still going up; but, in fact, they were coming down. I had seen what I thought was the light reflecting on their tracks or route, which was just right on the high ridges toward the summit, about fifteen miles away.

Anyway the weather settled in and today it is worse and visibility is about 100 feet to 1000 feet with rain and fog. I talked to Cliff a couple of times and apparently the forecast is for several days of foul weather. After the second group of storms, I would be surprised to see the rest of the Colorado group coming back to Base Camp.

I had brunch with the Germans and we had a great time. Herbert is a salesman for climbing equipment, Huber apparently owns or manufactures Salewa climbing equipment, Gunter works for the Free State of Bavaria as a surveyor for large municipal types of construction, and Fritz works for the publication department of the Chamber of Commerce in Munich. Karl comes from Garmisch in Bavaria. They speak slightly different German and it is quite close to Austrian German. The Germans (Bavarians) have fantastic amounts of food, and so we ate and ate.

The Bavarians seem to be a happy group and surely are quite different from the Prussian type of German. These particular men, and especially Herbert and Huber are extremely strong. The last two have climbed in New Guinea and Herbert and Gunter climbed in Greenland together with the Scots. Herbert, who is Karl's friend, has climbed everywhere but China, and led a climb of McKinley two years ago.

Later, it is just pouring down rain. It's certainly nice to know the Bavarians are next door. The avalanches are rumbling and also the thunder is thundering. What weather! If the weather doesn't clear in a couple of days, Huber, the Salewa mountain climbing equipment manufacturer, wants to borrow *Stonehenge.* He can read and speak English quite well. Herbert might be interested in looking at *Freedom of the Hills,* since he can read and speak English to some extent. For Fritz I have a humorous guide book in English-German, and also the Japanese version (a gift from one of the Japanese lady climbers) of a guide book for tourists in Japanese, English, German, Italian and Russian. For Gunter, the surveyor, who can hardly speak any English, I have *The Math Entertainer* and my pocket calculator.

August 1. It is still raining this morning and it rained very hard last night. The ceiling started to lift to about 1000 feet around 8:00 last night. Visibility went down to 100 feet yesterday. This morning I called Cliff, and the weather is "crummy" in Talkeetna. The transmission was not too good and I spent about fifteen minutes transmitting a 10-word telegram in German to Cliff.

The only special things about today were that it was telegram day, and that I talked to the Bavarians for a couple of hours. Finally, I have completed, in six languages, the battery terminal connections: positive terminal, red wire, and negative terminal, black wire. This information I will put in a plastic sack and attach it to the battery in the radio tent. The Germans helped me with the German, of course. The languages are English, Spanish, Russian, Japanese, French and German. If this lousy weather continues, I'll try to get the Germans to help with a translation of the German version of how to operate the radio.

August 2. The weather has cleared, so I hope the Germans and I can get out today. I'll send this letter out with them, so it will be mailed. Hope to see you soon.

15

August 3. The Germans got out just before the storm came in again. The pilots tried to come back, but conditions were terrible. They were going to try today, but the storm was still here—rain, wind, fog and clouds.

Now I have no neighbors once again. The Bavarians were truly among the most delightful people I have met on the glacier.

Hopefully, I can fly out tomorrow. Now I can see blue sky once in awhile in the evening and the cloud layer does not seem as thick. On the other hand, the storm may just be bouncing around from one place to another.

I completed the instructions of how to operate the radio in Spanish today. The parties that are on the Mountain are Japanese and American, and the Japanese can read the English. I still do not know whether the next party is Spanish or Italian.

I sent my last two letters out with Fritz, who was the Chamber of Commerce man from Munich. After the Spanish, I started to complete my Russian. It will soon be getting darker. I certainly hope I can leave tomorrow as I have so much to do.

In 1964, of a party of 19, all but two made the summit, including Frances (second from right) and Al Randall (right) and Bob and Marie Working. Randall was leader, Working, assistant leader.

Chapter Three — 1978

"Galen has pulmonary edema, but not badly"

June 10. Arrived on the Kahiltna after taking Sgook over to Fran.

June 11. Party of eight from Wyoming came in; three from Pacific Lutheran came in to fly out, two English, one Canadian. The weather is starting to close in.

The Air Force is finishing up a very expensive maneuver. They had ten people on the mountain, five of whom had to be taken off. To remove their last camp tonight, they needed a very large plane and two helicopters. Their dinner consisted of pork chops, ice cream and cookies, according to returning climbers. Fortunately they got out before the storm broke.

Galen Rowell and his buddy came in. Galen has pulmonary edema, but not badly. Galen's mother, Margaret Avery, played in the Arian Trio on the radio in San Francisco in the 1920s and '30s. Galen heads expeditions and should have been a cellist, as his mother is. His friend Ned is a fine person and is doing work for the Norwegian government. They climbed from 10000 feet to the top in sixteen hours: a record I believe.

Also, a lone climber came in last night with a badly twisted knee: ligament and cartilage are injured. Radio communication is very difficult. The ex-radio man, Phil, is a very nice young man who went climbing. He wanted to bring his dog up here, too. He is taking pictures of avalanches and will produce a movie. Every year is different. Mostly I miss Sgook, and now I count the days before I see Sgook.

Charlie Porter is over on the Ruth Glacier. I hope to get to see Charlie, but don't know if he is coming over here before he leaves.

June 13. Snow, whiteout, and the radio doesn't work. I finally found that the antenna had been disconnected. I talked to Cliff at 8:00 p.m. when it started to clear and arranged for a 5:00 a.m. weather check. Phil put a splint on Scott Johnson's knee, which is badly injured. Galen's edema is much

17

better. They need to catch a plane for Oslo. The Englishman and Canadian need to get out. I talked to Cliff at 5:00 p.m. It was snowing, then raining and whiteout; bad weather in Talkeetna. I walked the airstrip and reset the flags. The guys took lots of pictures of me playing my violin on the glacier with Hunter in the background.

I miss Sgook. I hope Tlaaga is OK. He is the old black lab that is supposed to go to Bettles. I think Sgook is much better in Talkeetna with Fran Leon. I read another version of *Popul Vuh*, which is much better. Also *Storm Warning* by Higgins, who wrote *The Eagle has Landed*, and now am on *Lacandon Dream* (symbolism, Maya Country in Chiapas). Also, I am doing some Russian.

June 15.   Mrs. Ha is inviting me to dinner when I get back later. This is Mea's mother, the little Korean girl who is doing very well. Dr. Ha is the father and he, along with Dr. Lindig, are the outstanding bone surgeons in the Northwest.

Scott Johnson (with the bad knee) and I had an interesting discussion on mathematics. There are now eleven climbers waiting for Cliff and four for Jim to fly out. Phil is coming back to continue his film on avalanches. The weather is bad in Talkeetna and not good here.

Dear Daddy: I bought a Father's Day card for you and also one for David to give you. Both are in Fairbanks. I'm asking a climber from Pacific Lutheran College in Tacoma to buy you one and send it to you. The weather has been very difficult. It seems as if there are not as many climbers this year. Only Americans, one Englishman and one Canadian are here at base camp. The weather is cold and it snows quite a lot. If it ever warms up, the avalanches should be sensational. This is all for now. Happy Father's Day.

June 16.   It snowed about one and a half feet last night. I had trouble with the generator. Galen and Phil cleaned the contacts, which had oil on them.

June 17.   The weather was very bad. Climbers in Talkeetna were wanting to fly in; those who had completed their climbs were in Camp waiting to fly out. There are many Japanese and one Korean. I fed the Korean and two Japanese supper. One Japanese lady from the party that came down the Mountain gave me two pancakes and the two Japanese men gave me a Mochi cake and coffee.

June 18.   It snowed again last night and now the weather appears to be changing. The Japanese from Saga told me about the old counts in Japan and how they used the moon counts as the base count. When he returns to Japan, he will send me the moon counts. There are now twenty-two here waiting to fly out and ten more coming down the Mountain. Right now Ryo-ji is writing a letter in Japanese to my friend, Tamae Watanabe, in Japan for me. Then I hope he will write one to Seigo Bando. They should be astonished to receive letters from me in Japanese. We all worked on the airstrip today and have all traded books; some people have read books twice. The Japanese set up a little ski race course today and raced to pass the time. The Korean seems very much alone. He speaks both a little English and much Japanese, but still he is very much alone. His two friends are in Talkeetna.

June 20.   I was on the radio at 4:00 a.m. and we started flights as soon as it cleared and the wind died down. About fifteen more came in for Genet, five from Osaka and five from Tokyo. The other two Koreans came in and then they all flew out, as they were doing a reconnaissance for a climb next year. They were very appreciative of my hospitality and gave me a beautiful banner. The Koreans were the first ones from their country and are very different from the Japanese. I told them about my violin students and they were very interested. I also talked to a Japanese student who is getting his PhD in chemistry from Ottawa, and told him about Yoshi. Twenty-two flew out today and five more from *Tokyo Alpine* came down from the summit, as did ten from *RMI*. The Japanese parties and I checked out their CB sets with mine.

Sometimes I give the pilots weather reports prior to final approval for landing or they give me messages about the people going out. I ran the generator for a couple of hours today (to charge the big battery), collected garbage, and got people out to the plane for flying out, greeted newcomers and did a million things. The weather and mountains were beautiful after the long storm. Cliff brought the letter from you that was written June 9. I'll read it many times since I didn't have my mail forwarded to Talkeetna and I have no other mail. All for now, as I must get some sleep.

June 21.   Five Japanese and ten Americans came down last night, and between Mike, Doug and Cliff they all got out. Four members of the NPS (one I know from last year) and ten climbers from Kobe who had tried to do Hayes (had bad weather) came in. The Kobe climbers knew of me. They have only nine days in this country. Five plan to do Crosson and five plan to try the West Buttress. We are also expecting some climbers from white South Africa. The NPS people came over for tea, ice cream and graham crackers and we talked for a long time.

Later, 10:00 p.m. On the first day of their climb, the four-man party from Kobe attempting Crosson had one person fall into a crevasse (the leader of the party, an older man, is in camp). Osaka climbers made their last carry today from base, as did the Tokyo climbers who are doing the West Rib. The latter is a party of five including one lady who borrowed my sewing kit to repair a ski binding. Then the French guide came by on his last carry. We talked for some time. I tried a little French and it came more easily than Japanese, which I hear continuously. Jim (pilot), Phil (photographer) and I all speak Spanish. Phil and I agree that if we are around Japanese enough, we could begin to pick it up. Weather continues to be terrible. Avalanche conditions continue to get worse. I practiced my violin last night and am doing Russian. There is no one in camp except me and the old man from Kobe.

June 24. The seven Japanese on the Cassin route of McKinley came back in the middle of the night. They were successful and are very tired. Later, Jack, the Frenchman, came back in a storm for more food and brought a message that two climbers, from Charlie Campbell's *North Star Expedition,* were returning to base camp. One of their members is extremely ill at 17300 feet. Howard Weaver and Kevin King got into base camp around 5:00 a.m., just before the Frenchman left. The climber at 17300 feet is near death. He was having severe headaches, then became delirious, dizzy and disoriented. This is another high altitude malady of which little is known. To save the rest of the party, five came down to a lower elevation. The leader stayed with the victim, Charlie Prentice. Five Japanese are there and the *Skinner Brothers* party of eight, from Wyoming and Colorado, are trying to reach 17300 feet.

I finally got through to Cliff. Communications are almost dead part of the time in this storm, as snow often carries high charges. Communication is extremely difficult, but I finally got the message through of the location of the climber, the name of the party, the weather conditions locally and on the Moun-

20

tain, and the condition of the climber. Cliff called back, saying they will send a helicopter as soon as possible. With these storm conditions, flying is impossible. The Kobe party on Crosson returned to the Crosson base where they talked to Edwards. I sent a note with the Frenchman to the four park rangers on the Mountain (who should be above 10000 feet now) regarding the Kobe climbers on Crosson. Fred Howard and Kevin came from 17300 feet with only one food stop and another coffee stop, with the Japanese from Tokyo (West Rib), to get here.

June 25. The winds up high have been terrible. The Charlie Campbell group lost their cook tent and the wind almost wiped out their other tents. They had to move to igloos and snow caves. I'll talk to Howard and Kevin when they get up. They are extremely exhausted. A party on the Mountain has almost no battery power left and they can only receive, so I am transmitting blind to them four times a day.

I'm monitoring the Kobe and Japanese group on Channels 2 and 6 and monitoring Channel 19 for American parties on CB. I talk to Cliff on high frequency (HF) of 3411 and to incoming pilots on CB 19 to advise them of wind or snow conditions. I talked to Cliff at noon and 4:00 p.m. via relay from Hayes River. Communication problems everywhere are very bad.

June 26. Around 2:20 a.m. five climbers from the Campbell party came in and I gave them hot Jell-o and cocoa. They are from the party with the ill climber, Charlie Prentice. The leader, Charlie Campbell, stayed with Prentice. Now everyone on the Mountain knows. The *Skinner* party is heading up and the French guide got the word to the rangers first. Later, I tried to call Cliff; communications are almost dead because of the highly-charged snow and atmosphere. Later in the morning, there were some signs of clearing and I got everyone out to do the runway. There won't be any communication until 4:00 a.m. and 8:00 a.m. Cliff came in around 9:30 a.m. and got four Japanese out under marginal weather. He tried again to get the rest out, but could not. Last night the temperature dropped many degrees within a few moments and the radio went absolutely dead. Helicopters came in to get ill Charlie, but were unsuccessful. They came back again after Cliff came in, but again were unsuccessful. At least now there is a lot of support up high. The Campbell party members that came down were weak, which is why the leader had them come down. Six Japanese stayed. Later around 10:30 a.m., three Japanese from this team came in. They now have the *Skinner* party, several Japanese parties and the NPS in the area.

I received your letter, and now I can read two letters for days.

June 27. Everybody that needed to go flew out and they got Charlie Prentice off the Mountain. Three of the Japanese from Osaka, who had been left here yesterday got out.

June 28. The five from South Africa came in. The four park rangers (Steve, Pete, Gretchen and Bill) came back and we discussed the rescue. The four from Kobe on Crosson came back with no mishaps. The *Edwards* party starts up Crosson tonight. Yesterday, three Kobe members came back from the West Buttress. Two are still trying for the top. Then three from Colorado, six from Calgary, five from Anchorage and other parts, three from Nevada, some from Durango, Colorado, two from Spokane (they know Eddie B. as his brother is in the Spokane Mountaineers). There must be a hundred and fifty on the Mountain. I had cooked moose for myself, then had Rosboosh tea with the South Africans. They are nice and very interesting people. English is their second language; their first language is a mixture of German, Holland Deutsche, French, English, African and Malaysian. Their names are Eknert, Kaas, Tammy, Clyde and Denne. Denne is a lady correspondent and has never been any place like this before.

Kitty, the lady pilot for Jim Sharpe, brought me some bread. Jim brought a huge chunk of salmon, Cliff brought some moose and Howard and Kevin sent me frozen chicken. Today was like Christmas. Then I had a huge meal with the Japanese from Kobe. Now they want to fly out and the weather looks terrible. Jim just got his last climbers in at midnight. The snow and rain have come back and the Japanese from Kobe want to go home.

This place looked like all of Talkeetna moved up here. I guess there were climbers camped out everywhere in Talkeetna waiting to fly in during the bad weather. Mike Fisher, who flies for both Cliff and Jim, got stuck over on the Ruth Glacier for six days with Charlie Porter. I guess Mike was happy enough as Charlie is great fun to be with. Charlie has now left the Mountain, as they finally got in to get Mike's plane off the glacier. The Kobe people are really depressed now.

June 29. It snowed all day. The South Africans plan to go to their next camp tomorrow night.

June 30. It snowed all night. I heard the South Africans returning from their carry to their next camp. I talked to the three members from the Japanese team (six) who helped Charlie Campbell at 17300 feet. They are in base. Snow and more snow, but the forecast is for clearing. I am enclosing Ros-boosh tea from South Africa, which I'll make when I get down there. Denne interviewed me today and took pictures of me skiing and then playing my violin on the Kahiltna.

July 1.   Looks like good weather for a few hours. Everybody got out and worked on the runway, except Phil, Wolfgang (who probably has a hairline fracture in his ankle) and John (who has some stomach malady.) The Japanese from Tokyo gave me a whole lot of cookies, Mochi (rice cakes), candy and a beautiful small towel. Cliff took out Wolfgang and two Kobe climbers. He tried to come in a second time, got within five miles last night about 9:00 p.m., and the weather turned. I talked to him on the CB while he was in flight. Part of the way is critical and the fog and cloud patterns were changing constantly.

July 2.   The weather-check at 6:00 a.m. revealed it's OK here, but not out in the foothills. Cliff tried to come in around 11:00 a.m. and had to turn back ten miles out. Later, everyone got out leaving only some baggage, Phil and Doogal. One Japanese man from Nara came in and, about 10:20 p.m., nine climbers came in. They had walked forty miles, mostly in the rain, from Petersville up the Kahiltna. They brought me a message from an old prospector at Cache Creek (who acts as a relay to Talkeetna sometimes) that he had been trying to get me on the radio. I knew the leader from last year; he is from Boston and his name is Phil. I made them hot Jell-o.

July 3.   Rain, rain, snow all day. Ryoji spent about an hour on Japanese with me. The *Infinite Odyssey* group needs food, so I have been trying since 4:00 a.m. to get hold of Cliff. We talked at 8:00 a.m., 12:00 a.m. and again at 4:00. p.m. Communications now are almost impossible with the storms.

July 4.   It snowed last night; clearing today. Doug came in twice and Jim once. *Infinite Odyssey* never got their groceries. They miscalculated on amounts. I got the call through to Hayes River and then on to Cliff. The weather cleared for a few hours only. It just finished sleeting, the wind is blowing and huge air masses are moving overhead. Conditions high up must be atrocious. One party of four came in today from Talkeetna; their call sign is *Fireworks*. I talked to them tonight. They are on the east fork of the Kahiltna now. They informed me that a party of three was coming in with one member who has bronchitis. The one-man Japanese team woke me up at 5:45 a.m. to give me breakfast of noni (cubes of some sort of fish) and mushrooms, which he apparently had started preparing while visiting with other people until 1:00 or 2:00 this morning. I couldn't imagine this beautifully prepared dish on a beautiful flowered paper plate, steaming food and covered with sani-wrap.

Base Camp at any hour never seems to be dull and I surely never know what may happen next. People drag in any time. By now I really do not know what is going on outside. I hope to get off soon if the weather permits at the proper time. I haven't heard from anyone else but you; from your letters it sounds like you haven't received but one or two of mine and I have now sent five. I keep track of the dates.

July 5. Last night the Genet group of seven came in and also Ron Cratzer from Colorado. Ron radioed out from 19000 feet and found he had to return to Base and get over to Africa. He was the head of teaching the Nigerians how to drill oil and now their government is taking over. Finally, by noon, I got through to Grandview and Hayes River with a critical message to get in touch with Jim Sharpe to either fly in or bring a 206 helicopter to get him out. Jim Reed, the man with bronchitis, was on the team with several other guys. One of them, Les Snick, is a well-known climber and was slated to go to Russia on an exchange. Also Craighead is along, and his brother, or father, or family do National Geographic articles on wildlife. Jim's condition is OK, but it could go into pneumonia or edema immediately, so I cooked for him and talked to him a lot. He gave me his team T-shirt, which is a beautiful silk screen. Also Jim's wife's older sister lives on the Hudson in N.Y., and arranges recitals at Carnegie, so I'm writing Jean.

The weather keeps looking like it will clear, but the fog keeps hanging in. If it ever clears in the next few days, I'll fly out I guess, as Kevin (Billy's brother) is ready to come in as soon as I leave. Depending on how long I have, I will give two sets of violin lessons when I return to Fairbanks, then go to Anchorage to pick up my good violin and attend to some business before returning to Fairbanks. I'll leave my car in Talkeetna and pick it up later.

July 7. It snowed last night. Today I worked on the runway. The weather lifted for a few hours. Jim came in, but couldn't land, as the fog was about fifty feet above Camp. He landed down glacier about five miles. Then Cliff came by and

24

the fog lifted enough to land. Cliff brought the food for *Infinite Odyssey*. Finally, Jim was able to come in, but the glacier where he had landed earlier was soft and he had to leave two climbers down there with gear. They pushed and got the plane off the ground. (We frequently have to push or help turn the plane around. As it gets going, you fall to one side to miss the tail.) After one track was made, Cliff went down and picked up the two climbers. Finally, the bronchitis-case (whom I had looked after for one and one-half days), Ron with the drilling problems in Nigeria, and Don from N.Y. (part of *Odyssey* who didn't make the top), and Genet's seven got off from base, while ten from *RMI* flew in (one was from Vancouver, B.C.). Tracy Roberts (leader) came in and remembered me from when he was here before. Later, the *Skinner* party came in. They traveled heavy like Al and I used to travel. Courtney Skinner, I believe, is from the big Skinner Corporation. I never know who I will meet next.

During all of this activity, Jim Hale, one of the guides on the Mountain, wanted to know the forecast, *Durango* wondered if Mike Bradley got to camp because of his altitude problems, and *Infinite Odyssey* asked if the food arrived. Then on the next-to-last trip Jim came in to take the rest of the *Skinner* party and Mike out. He stuffed five people plus himself into the Cessna 185 and barely got off. Later he came back and brought a 10-foot high birch tree, some bread, grape juice, lime sherbet and moose meat. We took pictures of the tree, which seems incredibly out of place on the glacier. This is the second time in twenty-eight days that I've seen something green, as one climber brought a little plant.

July 8. I got up at 4:00 a.m. to get two remaining members of *Infinite Odyssey* up, as they wanted to start up the hill with the food. I have the only alarm clock here. Terrible storms have been predicted, but so far the weather has been nice; probably the calm before the storm. There was a fantastic avalanche on Foraker. Hunter still has not avalanched and it's scary. Communications today are impossible, which further indicates terrible storms. High winds in the afternoon, then calm. Cliff brought in two guys later.

July 9. Nice weather. Cliff brought in four and Sharpe brought in one. I'm supposed to go out tomorrow. Later, ten Japanese from Nakamura came back; two on the summit. Now I am number eleven to go out.

July 10. Weather is bad, but it finally cleared enough for Cliff to take out eight Japanese. Jim took out Genet and Fenden. Also fixed frostbitten feet of Frenchman Joe.

July 11. Cliff came in twice. Two from Nakamura, Ryoji and I flew out on the final flight. The weather was jumpy in the keyhole.

A visit from Ollie Hudson, wife of bush pilot Cliff Hudson, and dog.

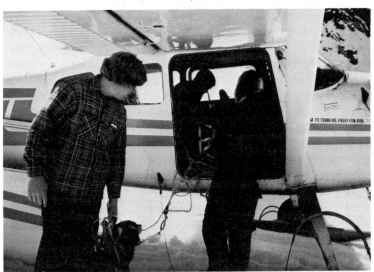

Loading dogs onto plane on Kahiltna Glacier.

Chapter Four — 1979

Hypothermia, shock, frostbite, and two fatalities

May 28. Flew in. Beautiful day. A Korean party (seven members) starts to come in today.

May 29. Bad weather. Some snow.

May 30. Snowed at night. I established contact with a Korean party on the West Rib at 16000 feet while I was checking out the radio equipment on a channel with the Korean party in camp. The party on the Mountain is composed of six members; three reached the summit yesterday. Four are from Korea, one is Korean-American and one is American. About 10:30 a.m., while monitoring my regular Channel 19, I received a message of an emergent nature to monitor Channel 1. I talked to the Korean party on the Mountain and they stated that they thought they had a problem and needed to have Cliff contacted and asked to monitor Channel 1.

Soon the three Korean party members who had reached the summit reported that they saw six or seven people walking to 14000 feet. Then we heard of one fatality. Korean party members finally reached 14000 feet. In the meantime, a C130 Air Rescue plane came in and started "orbiting" (their terminology) over camp at 14000 feet. I made radio contact with Air Rescue and continued to monitor the operation and assist when necessary, as two park rangers were at Base Camp at the time. There was no other radio at 14000 feet until the Korean party arrived. Then we heard of two fatalities and one seriously injured climber who had a dislocated right knee, hypothermia, shock, abdominal pain and third-degree frostbite. Around 1:30 p.m. two Chinooks (high altitude Air Force helicopters from Wainwright—one was a back up) came in and the pickup was made. Later I learned that the Chinook landed in Talkeetna and couldn't fly, so the injured party was reevacuated to Elmendorf Hospital.

The seven Korean members in Base Camp (from another expedition) waited until the evacuation off the Mountain was completed before they departed to do the West Buttress. Later in the evening, people started coming into Camp and I learned more details.

The rangers flew out as soon as they could since they had work to do and had to report conditions on the Mountain. The *Anchorage Community College* and *Genet* parties at 14000 feet had seen, at about 8:30 last night, what looked like a rock falling down the West Buttress from about 2000 feet above them and Genet concluded they had better go take a look. They found one fatality. Since they could bring only one person back at a time, they brought the one who was in the best condition. They left the other in a snow cave and it did not look like he would survive as his head injuries were severe. When they got back, he had died.

Meanwhile, I heard that the dog mushers are coming down. Weather was marginal in Base Camp, but finally cleared and people were flown out.

May 31. Weather was beautiful when I awoke. A little later, dog teams arrived with Genet, a photographer, Joe Reddington and Susan Butcher. The latter two are both Iditarod racers (that's the 1000-mile race from Anchorage to Nome). Joe has been a winner and Susan has placed 10th, I think; she is the only woman to win money. The dogs were beautiful and apparently had learned about being belayed up fixed rope. All in all, it was quite an experience. It was quite a sight to see a dog sled loaded in a Cessna 185, but when the second dog sled, seven dogs, Joe and Susan, plus Doug the pilot, were all in one 185, that was a real sight. The dogs are remarkably good, and when they are packed in a plane, dogs that ordinarily don't get along, do. They seem to adopt the attitude that they all must suffer this thing out together. When they get out of the plane it seems to practically explode, as the dogs apparently are so happy to have it over. Some dogs seem to like to fly and watch the scenery, but others do not.

After all of that was over, people flew out all day long. Oh yes, yesterday, two young Germans from Munich came in to climb the West Buttress with little equipment and left immediately. The other day I talked to another German who was leaving; he lived near Munich.

In the afternoon I reset the landing flags on the lower strip. Pete Sennhauser, from Anchorage, Gunnar and Vahn discussed what they should climb—maybe Foraker. Vahn, also from Anchorage, plays cello and knows a lot of the same musicians I do. He went to the University of Alaska and graduated this last year in chemistry at Fairbanks. Our paths have never crossed before (he didn't play in the University of Alaska Symphony, but did play in the Anchorage Symphony when he was there. We have had very interesting discussions.

Two people came in late last night. I talked to three Japanese from Kitakyushushi and they are going to do the West Buttress instead of the West Ridge of Hunter as it is very heavily crevassed and has horrendous overhanging cornices.

June 1.   Doug flew in and took out two people. This is the first day that I haven't been so busy. At 4:18 p.m. I received a Mayday call from 14000 feet. I tried to contact Talkeetna, then Roy, then *Lady Sunflower*. I got a response from *Lady Sunflower*. Doug is in the near vicinity, finally.

6:05 p.m. Doug is burning off gas in order to land at 10000 feet. The weather is deteriorating, but will probably hold.

6:07 p.m. Doug tried to land.

6:15 p.m. He's on the ground. I talked to Jim Hale, a guide I've known for a long time; he helped bring the injured person down.

6:33 p.m. Doug is weathered in, but it's still OK here.

6:49 p.m. *Cascade Denali* called; I advised them to call after 8:30.

7:12 p.m. Doug took off; he's low on fuel, and has an elevator problem. I'll continue to monitor Doug.

7:19 p.m. Roy picked up and monitored Doug to Talkeetna; a medical technician will be needed for the injured person.

8:05 p.m. Doug is in Talkeetna.

June 2.   I established contact with Roy on the HF. Then I rechecked the equipment and discovered that the antenna needs to be connected from control to the transmitter. During morning check in, I can hear Eskimos all along the West Coast, and Wien Airlines in Bethel. I received an urgent message from Roy this afternoon to advise climbers of extremely high winds and deteriorating weather coming in. I talked to both Korean parties and Steve at 15500 feet, and to the Williamson party at 17000 feet. Later there were high winds, but no problem here.

June 3.   Mike Kennedy, two Swiss, Vahn, and four Japanese from Tokyo (who were unsuccessful on Cassin) went out. Harry and Young Chou brought Mr. Kim down. Mr. Kim is from the Korean Times, which has changed its sponsorship

29

to their Everest climber and two others plus Mr. Kim. Young Chou speaks excellent English and has a B.S. in computer science. Young Chou knew of Dr. Ha. Harry and Young Chou went back to 9000 feet to pick up gear. Pete Sennhauser and Gunnar (from Anchorage) left for Foraker. Weather is deteriorating.

June 4. Up early. Practiced my violin. Mugsy came in. I must go back to work. *Lady Sunflower* apparently has no bear problem now. I saw a little sparrow during the past week and a little junco has been here, too. I've put out bacon grease and bread crumbs. Then a beautiful little yellow warbler stopped. I haven't seen the junco today. It usually comes right up to the tent. I received your letter, and thank you. I really appreciate them up here. I've been here about a week, and there has been some sort of crisis almost every day. Since few people are roping up on the glacier these days, and the crevasses are opening up, and snow conditions are constantly changing, there will probably be more trouble.

9:30 p.m. Well, the crisis for today is bad weather. The report was relayed from Anchorage and they want a weather report from here due to extremely unstable conditions. Around 3:00 p.m. the weather was clearing but then it hit. Usually we do not have winds like that here; the tent was in the way but other items weren't touched.

Two Americans and a Scot came down. I talked to Young Chou and nine others (also at 17200 feet) with the Williamson party to get news on the Mountain. Yesterday, I found out that the cyclic radio, which occurs once in awhile and is very disturbing, is interference from Russian radar. Roy told me that (he's a radio expert at Montana Creek).

Oh yes, here's what happened when the wind hit. It blew in one end of the tent, tipped over two stoves and a pan of boiling water, which fell into a lemon pie mix and crust that a climber and I had decided to make — it was just about done. He had had the graham crackers, butter and sugar, and I had had eggs, powdered milk, sugar and lemon pie mix. After cleaning up and securing the tent, we ate the pie anyway. It was OK, even if it was soggy and runny.

The wind calmed down again. There are supposed to be ten climbers waiting to come in. Twice, I talked to Pete over at the foot of Foraker. Contact is very good. Between all the rumpus of the day, I read and worked on math too. What a day! I hope I never have another lemon pie like that.

June 5. It was calm in the morning and now winds have picked up. Visibility is OK, but winds are now gusting over 20 knots. It may clear out in the afternoon. I practiced my violin this morning and then someone knocked on the tent. Pete and Gunnar had returned from Foraker. Weather is just bad. Two Americans and a Scot came down.

11:00 p.m. Wind, snow, clearing.

4:00 a.m. No plane. Talked to Cliff at 2:00 p.m.

June 6. It snowed last night. I'm having battery problems. I recharged the big battery twice, fixed the battery clamp, and used the small emergency battery to get through. Whiteout, winds calm. Steve, at 16400 feet, called to say he is coming down.

June 7. The battery problem has been solved except it takes a long time to charge the big battery. I repaired the charger clamp. Bad weather. Three Japanese, who were going to do Hunter and then McKinley, returned. One has had snow blindness and they look depressed. They must be successful if they want further sponsorship, I think. I talked a long time to Young Chou and then had rice and bean paste with them. Delicious! I surely like Oriental food. Korean is very hot. *Cascade Denali* (four) came in and they did not make the summit, as Steve, the leader, became very sick over 17200 feet. They said how much they really liked talking to me on the radio as they had no other contact. Weather is bad.

June 8. Four Swiss climbers came in last night. I talked to Cliff at 7:00 a.m. Weather might clear in the afternoon and it should be good tomorrow. I'm reading *View Over Atlantis* and it has a lot more about all the old sites in England, Wales, Ireland and Scotland. Fascinating book. I must turn off the generator now. The weather is good enough to fly—marginal, but OK. Cliff has twenty climbers to come in. So far six from Oregon, six from Montana, more Germans and Swiss to come. Out of necessity, I start talking German, but my Japanese has almost left me. I learned some Korean from Young Chou and have spent some time to get the right pronunciation of important words.

The last trip Cliff made in, he said Jim Hale was bringing a pulmonary edema victim down the Mountain from 17200 feet. Jim, whom I have known for years, is one of the top guides.

I talked to him briefly when Doug came in to pick up the victim with the broken ankle. I also talked to Jim several times the last few days on the radio. Right now there is a little lull for a few minutes. I received two letters from you, one dated June 4, and this is the eighth of June. The weather is not right to pick up the pulmonary edema victim that Jim Hale and two others are bringing down. Cliff is flying over and talking to the victim's party and to Base. Three from Base went out to meet the victim and the assistant leader from Jim Hale's party.

June 9.   I monitored the radio until 4:30 a.m. The Williamson party returned from the summit. They were at least 3000 feet below Jim. At about 7:30 a.m., the three from Base, the assistant leader, and the pulmonary edema victim came into Camp. I talked to Cliff. The weather is clear, but there is some wind.

I received a message from Jim Hale (who is back at 15000 feet and climbing) that there is one sick German at 14200 feet who is being helped by *Denali Sports*. Two Germans are missing. They were last seen at 11:00 a.m. yesterday at 19000 feet with ski poles but no ice axes, no food or water, and in poor condition. One German, who had been at 19000 feet, is now at Denali Pass. Jim Hale's party is investigating. A visual distress signal was seen at 8:00 a.m. today. A high overflight is needed. I finally contacted someone on the CB and also Hayes River. Flight Service located Cliff. I talked on HF 3411 and got some information: The military has been alerted and a helicopter is to take off for 14200 feet and will probably drop a radio at Denali Pass. The weather is still holding, but may change. By 8:40 a.m., the helicopter (high altitude) had arrived from Talkeetna and brought down the German with pulmonary edema from 14200 feet. It then went back to Denali Pass and picked up two more. One was fine and came along, I think, to interpret. The other was in serious condition. What a day! Poor Jim Hale has to climb up the Mountain again.

June 10.   Wind, snow, rain last night, whiteout. I heard from Roy that the prediction is for heavy snow and high winds for the next twenty-four hours or longer. Jim Hale called for a weather report earlier. He's at 16000 feet and going up. He has been going up and down that Mountain ever since I've been here.

June 11.   Bad weather continues, extremely high winds, clear high. Went skiing with Valentin Demmel while the battery recharged. Since he knows almost no English, we spoke German, and I don't know how I manage because I speak limited German. The winds are terrible up high and extremely high for here. I have not heard from the Koreans for days. Nor have I heard from Jim Hale, Simo (Eric Simonson of one *RMI* group), Phil Ershler (another *RMI* group), or other groups on the Mountain. So, I don't know what happens next. Weather predictions are bad.

June 12. Winds continue to be terrible. Four guys came from the Ruth Glacier and are continuing down the Kahiltna. They were held up in the Ruth Gap for thirty-six hours and one tent was nearly demolished. Brian and two from Talkeetna are going up the Southeast Fork to Peak 12380. I finally heard from Phil, who is across the Kahiltna at the foot of Crosson. I also received a weather report that we may have decreasing winds in the next twenty-four hours, but maybe more snow. The top of McKinley is like a great white feather with extremely high winds carrying the snow many miles into the sky.

I thought I heard a bit of Russian radar again, but I guess it's other atmospheric conditions. I heard Savoonga on St. Lawrence Island yesterday. (Interior Alaska has many forest fires). I practiced my violin this morning and the German was so happy, as one of his children plays the violin. He is fixing the rain fly on my tent. I cook for him as he has no food or stove. Brian is neighbors with some people who are friends of the Chapins (who are keeping Sgook) in Fairbanks.

June 13. Weather is marginal. The *Genet* party is flying out with Doug. Last evening I talked with the remainder of the *Denali Sports* group from Everett, Washington. One is a pediatrician in Anchorage with Alaska Native Hospital. They have now flown out. Today I talked with Victor, who has a probable broken bone in his foot, from the Crosson-Foraker Traverse. He is from San Francisco and was with Phil Ershler from *RMI*. Victor lost his entire family (except for his immediate family), in a quick departure from Germany in 1942. We talked until his plane took off. Then I talked some more with Rick Graetz *Montana Magazine* publisher and manager/owner) and Fred Flanders (president of the Montana State Bank), both of Helena, and with Leon Odegaard from Billings. They are with Ray Genet. I also met a PE teacher from Nome who had heard the Arctic Chamber Orchestra. Fred had heard the Spokane Symphony and was very interested in Spokane.

Chris Landry turned back from his solo climb of the West Rib and came in with the four English. We talked about climbing before his plane left. A lot of these climbers are heading for Leavenworth. Ray Genet finally has some twenty-two or twenty-three people that Doug has flown in. Jim Sharpe had problems with his hydraulic system and had to go get it fixed. I finally got your letter and I guess you must have gotten the information about the Korean mishap. There is now a Dr. Kim Sang Soo with Ray Genet. Sang Soo did a lot of mountaineering in Korea and then did his internship and residency in Kentucky and now he is able to do some mountaineering again. Today the weather was sort of marginal. Talked to Roy about the weather. He phones in weather reports to Anchorage that I give to him from here, and then Anchorage compiles a report for the Mountain. I hope Daddy got his Fathers' Day present that I sent months ago and the card I sent from here.

June 14. Three Germans from Garmisch came in yesterday. They saw Karl in Garmisch and then stopped and visited with Ann and Mark in Anchorage. Genet's party of twenty-seven took off in the afternoon. Genet will probably come in tomorrow. Cliff brought in two frozen chickens. He also brought in three Japanese teams and finally got Ed off the Tokositna Glacier. It's very tricky flying over there. I could transmit, so, when the weather cleared late in the day, Ed called me and I got hold of Cliff. I talked to Cliff both in the air and when he finally got down on the strip that Ed had marked (lighting is very bad in the late evening). Cliff got off about 11:00 p.m.

Alan and John came down. They had helped with some of the rescues. Alan is from England and is very strong. Most of the climbers stayed in snow caves at Denali Pass during the extremely high winds.

June 15. Alan and John flew out. There is no one in Camp except for two Japanese teams who should be leaving again when the snow gets cold. Genet is supposed to come in this evening. Weather is deteriorating. I got some fresh tomatoes, onions, radishes, cucumber, lettuce and hamburger. Later, Brian Okonek, Mark and Art came in from Peak 12380. They were thirty-six hours on the ascent-descent of this very impressive mountain at the head of the southeast fork of the Kahiltna. They had saved some fresh meat and made a stew with some sort of spaghetti combination on top. They also brought buns and brownies. I made a fresh salad, and we had popcorn for dessert. What a fantastic meal! We talked about climbing, as they knew a lot of people I know and vice versa. We all agreed that we liked the dogs and dog mushers. I heard from the Korean team, the NPS and *RMI*.

June 16. Whiteout and wet snow. Talked to Cliff, Roy and Genet's party. Got the weather report and prepared a Japanese version. A Mexican team is supposed to be coming. Practiced my violin. Later, two members of the Korean team reached the summit. I sent a weather report in Japanese to the *Iwatoyuki* team on the West Buttress.

June 17. A telegram arrived from Korea, via Mr. Kim in Anchorage, for the Korean team on the Mountain. Also, I sent a telegram via Cliff to Korea. Light, wet snow with a ceiling at 8000-9000 feet. Local light fog and calm winds. I talked to Roy for a few minutes. Genet called and hired Brian and Art to go up and help his team of twenty-seven.

June 18. Weather outside of here is not good. Several flew out. Several flew in. Ray Genet came in and a lady and baby are going part way up (the baby likes it).

6:30 p.m. Talked to NPS and Koreans at 12000 feet, and others. They all yelled to me over the radio, "Hi Frances" from 12000 feet down to here. It is weathering in again. Three arrived from Seattle. I expect the eight Swiss to come down. Last night I dreamed that the Koreans gave me a huge ivory cat in a sitting position and a live kitten. Later, the NPS came in and the eight Swiss arrived. One is actually Canadian and one is from Liechtenstein.

The Koreans are not here. They are very tired. Then I heard that one has bad frostbite and they decided to thaw his feet with boiling water, spilled the water, and scalded the feet of another climber. According to NPS they do not want help. Another group saw four start off with light packs from 8000 feet to come here. I talked to Cliff.

June 20. The Koreans still are not here. It's snowing, whiteout, winds are calm. I talked to Cliff. Hope the Koreans are OK. We have enough support here to help, but they do not want help, due to the bad publicity it would create for their country. So we wait. The NPS, several strong Americans and the Swiss team are here. The Swiss are very strong. I took their pictures, we traded Swiss chocolate and moose sausage (Cliff brought me some). The Liechtensteiner gave me a pennant (beautiful). The Koreans arrived late. We served hot chocolate and tea. The Swiss had tea ready too. We built, with help from the Swiss team, platforms on the ice for the Korean huts. The Austrian in the Swiss team did a beautiful architecture job. The Koreans gave us candies, dried fish, etc. Earlier Mike from NPS and I took a ski tour down glacier to check weather in the lower foothills and see if we could spot the Koreans up the glacier. Dave (NPS) watched the radio. We had a nice tour, ate a Washington apple and watched avalanches.

June 22. Beautiful weather. The Swiss team is very happy. They organized a climb in Switzerland. The eight members consisted of four Swiss, one Liechtensteiner, two East Germans (one spoke Spanish so we conversed in that, as it was easier with my poor German and his poor English), and one Austrian. The variety of German languages makes it difficult to settle on one. Here there was Swiss German, East German (which sounded like Low German), the Liechtenstein version of German, and Austrian German. German also changes towards the French border and Bavarian German is again different. With four versions at the same time, it's hard to learn anything. We all took pictures. The Americans gave a birthday party for an older man from Tucson with their canned fruit cake and a plumber's candle they borrowed from me. They all took pictures and I played my violin with everybody photographing. Then the man from Liechtenstein yodeled. It was beautiful. The Koreans and I took pictures. The day was beautiful.

During last night, nineteen people who had walked up the glacier (40 miles) came in. One young kid had been sick for ten days, vomiting blood. He went out on the first plane with NPS. I relayed a message to Cliff to make a collect call to Palmer for someone to meet the sick person.

At 8:20 a.m., John at 17,200 feet called about one sick Icelander. He and one other Montana person stayed behind with the sick Icelander—everyone else went to the top. I tried to get them to walk to lower elevation. Some medical technicians who had gone by said he doesn't have cerebral edema, though the symptoms are of cerebral edema. NPS (Dave) talked to them. Later, when transmission was bad, the summit teams came down and they decided not to move until the next morning. The weather was perfect (not a good decision to stay). Dave was disgusted earlier because of the medical technicians' diagnosis. He says, and I concur, that over fifty percent of professional medical assistance on the Mountain has been unsuitable or wrong. Two (Dave and Mike) from NPS flew out.

John from the Montana group called. The Icelanders want a helicopter for a rescue. I took down the symptoms and what manpower was there. Then, I got hold of Cliff, but couldn't reach the Park Service. I got back to John from the Montana group. They are going to get those Icelanders to walk. There is enough available manpower and weather is perfect. If weather socks in, there will be a real problem.

June 23. The Icelanders walked out and improved as they came down. Many people to fly in. Phil should be on top of the Crosson-Foraker traverse and, later, the summit of Foraker. Lowell Thomas, Jr. flew in and out. About 12:00 p.m., I received a call from the Montana group that a man is very sick. I arranged for a flight over the area.

1:10 p.m. Cerebral edema; three doctors were working with the victim.

1:15 p.m. Seizure. I tried to contact Cliff; I finally got him (through Bunco Lake to Talkeetna), and had him contact Providence in Anchorage. Jay came in with a Super Cub and dumped gas to fly up higher. From the monitor I learned that Cliff had landed. He had to land twice due to the bad condition of the snow. The evacuee was put on board. A medic (4th year medical student) was here to assist with the transfer to a 185. The victim could barely breathe with oxygen. He was flown straight to Providence in Anchorage, but he started to turn blue just before the ambulance arrived in Anchorage. Cliff came back with more people. Jan came in. Phil made the summit. What a day! I hope Jim lives. We surely tried. It came on suddenly.

I got a letter from Mother dated June 18, and one from Daddy dated June 19. Did you get the Father's Day sketch, Daddy? It's 11:25 p.m. and I'm writing, looking out at the sun's reflection touching the top of Mt. Foraker.

June 24. Whiteout. Wet snow and winds came. Phil, at 11400 feet at the foot of Foraker on the Foraker-Crosson traverse, reports high winds, 30-40 knots, gusting up to 60 knots. He is sitting it out. CEC called. (Mary borrowed my boots; this is their second time to the top.) Two Japanese groups called. More Japanese called. It's really a problem, when communications are bad, to hear English, let alone another language. There are five Japanese groups on the Mountain. I'm certainly learning about listening, and trying to sort out messages over radio noise is challenging. I listen for rhythm and sound patterns in speech.

June 25. Whiteout. Wet snow, about a foot new, slight winds (0-2 knots) from the Northeast. I do not know about two young men on Hunter. They were trying a very difficult route and if they have survived, I'm sure they are low on food. I talked to quite a few of the climbing groups, and at 8:00 a.m. it will be mostly Japanese. Cliff usually calls then, too. It was something when a Japanese team, a Korean team and Cliff all call at the same time. It has now dumped over several feet of snow and there is grave danger of flooding in the lowlands. The rivers and lakes are rising rapidly. Phil, over on Foraker, is OK. If this weather ever clears! Thank goodness, Cliff got that sick man off the Mountain in the nick of time. Cliff called the hospital yesterday, and he is out of intensive care.

June 26. Well, the storm continues. Almost three feet of new snow. Down low the rivers are starting to flood. Up here and higher it's bad weather. I am in contact with most groups on the Mountain. I'm alone now, but expect a party of three from Montana that is bringing in a member with a bad ankle. That should be late tonight. Now Phil can not move on the ridge with the six to eight feet of new snow, and they are out of food with hardly any fuel left. We should get one or two more feet of snow tonight and maybe some clearing before the next front moves in. Later, I heard from Phil; the wind has let up a little and they are sacking out. I just prepared the weather report in Japanese.

June 27. Phil called and requested a helicopter to get three off the traverse. They are at extreme risk with cold feet and being tired. From their symptoms, they seem to be in about the same condition that most of the climbers on Pinnacle Peak were in. I called out and NPS finally approved. A helicopter finally came up. It was light. One small dot was visible on the ridge, probably ten miles away at 11200 feet. Weather started to close in. Later in the day it turned out better.

June 28. The Montana group was here and went out. They are very grateful for Jim's life being saved. Weather is pretty good.

June 29. Everybody that came down the Mountain has gone out. Morning weather was not good, but the afternoon was beautiful. I straightened the antennae. That takes at least four people. Five came in from Washington yesterday to do a route on the Southern Buttress. Two are from Roslyn or Cle Elum, two are from Alpental, and one is a dentist (new) from Wenatchee (his name is Dr. McFadder and he knows Dr. Smith at Leavenworth).

June 30.   Not much happened. Talked to Susan of *Infinite Odyssey.*

July 1.   Rescue in process: a pulmonary edema victim around 14000 feet. Jim landed this time. He had made an early flyover, and discovered a visual emergency signal on the ground. I did not contact him, as he is on a different channel. Russian radar is now interfering with the network and jamming. Jim is ready for the takeoff. The Japanese try to use this channel; in my limited Japanese, I tell them to wait. The kid from *Infinite Odyssey* who needs tetracycline for a staff infection finally got his prescription filled (cost $135.00 including air transport to Palmer with a doctor, taxi fare, telephone calls and cost of the medicine).

July 2.   Clear, beautiful morning. Lowell Thomas, Jr., was in and took the Genet party out. Ten Koreans came in with Cliff, then two more from Pittsburgh and finally three young men from Colorado. The French party came back to leave some bags and decided not to do the Crosson-Foraker traverse but, instead, to do the West Buttress and the traverse if there is time. We speak mostly Spanish, combined with French and English. The Mexicans are supposed to arrive tomorrow.

I received a letter and you said I had not written, but I write every day. It is always possible that the letter didn't get mailed. Anyway I surely receive more letters up here on the glacier than I did back in Fairbanks, which is OK, and your telephone bill should be considerably less now.

The man from Missoula had to go back to the hospital to intensive care, and I don't know how he is. His family is the Halls and one of them has an oriental restaurant there. It's been a long time since I've seen anything green. A letter postmarked June 28 arrived on the Kahiltna July 2.

July 3.   Five climbers from British Columbia (B.C.) flew in, and I found out that we know some of the same people in B.C. These men are from Vancouver. The Mexican team flew in. It's very hot. The skip is high in the radio; I'm getting interference from Russian radar.

July 4.   The Mexicans are from Mexico City and it turns out two had seen me at Socuro Alpino many years ago and we knew many of the same people, so this was a great day. The Canadians, Mexicans and I reset the antennae for the radio. It rained hard most of the day, but that seems to be a typical day on the glacier. I did not hear from the *SUWA* man. I arranged with the Koreans for them to listen to Channel 1 from 8:00-8:30 p.m. after this. I also advised Cliff of a potential problem on the West Rib.

July 5.   The Koreans left in the early morning. Fog. I heard from *SUWA* and *Iwatoyuki* at 10000 feet, also Korea. Now I am talking a little Korean, a little more Japanese, some German and Spanish. The Mexicans brought tapes, so I have their radio (AM/FM), which also is a tape cassette. It is a GE and very good, the Koreans called and asked about it.

July 6.   The Mexicans bought their GE radio and tape cassette at Jafco for sixty dollars. I lent the Mexicans my skis and found another pair, so they could try skiing; it was the first time for most of them. I eat with the Mexicans, or they always invite me. These men are from the University of Mexico and are either students or professors. Their climb is sponsored by the University and they are one of the best organized teams on the Mountain. They are interested in classical music, anthropology, climbing the ruins in Latin America and, since they are with the University of Mexico, they are more than willing to give me sources of information there.

July 7.   Lots of wind last night. Climbers were finally able to move on the Mountain. Conditions are clear. The Mexicans made a carry last night to Kahiltna Pass. The *Iwatoyuki* group of five, which includes two Japanese ladies from Osaka, came back. Weather cleared out and supposedly there will be several days of good weather before the next front comes in. Five Belgians came in. A party of six came in: four are from France and two are Swiss ladies (one a doctor and one a school teacher). Groups here now are mostly *Genet* groups. A *Genet* group is right next to me. It includes some people from Europe. Then there are also a bunch of people from the South. The French-Swiss party seems interesting and nice. The Swiss doctor had read about me somewhere. I've talked to Lowell Thomas a bit. He brings me newspapers, *Time Magazine* and fresh fruit. The Mexicans and I had quite a picture-taking session with lots of cameras. I also took many pictures with the Japanese group, *Iwatoyuki,* and with the Canadians before they left.

Jim Sharpe told me that there may be two fatalities in

Cathedral Spires. This party is supposedly from Washington. The Spires are a popular area southwest of here. Then Jeff from Bunco Lake (south of here in the tundra) called and said he heard an urgent call from a climber on the Mountain when I was out at the planes. I tried to locate him, but didn't make contact. I also talked to the Mexican team.

July 8. It snowed lightly in the morning. The *SUWA* group came in from the West Rib. Jim spotted two Japanese coming down from Hunter. They did the lower Kennedy route. Very difficult.

I don't know where I'll be on my birthday, but I should be down the Mountain by then. I ordered books from the Talkeetna Library and among the ones they sent were *Grimm's* and *Andersen's Fairy Tales,* so I read them. I skimmed through a few novels and also started *Psychic Discoveries Behind the Iron Curtain,* which I got from Cathleen and Steve. The weather is terrible and there is a terribly sick climber coming down. This weather has been terrible. Sometimes I wonder if I shall ever leave, but I'm better off than the sick climber coming down the Mountain.

July 9. Fifteen years ago today I climbed the Mountain, and I just found out that my boots made it to the summit again two days ago.

The weather! It snowed again last night. Whiteout in the morning. The sick man is at 16200 feet. He can't make progress down because of the storm. It started to lift. I heard from Bob Cooper (with the group that has my boots). A Japanese

man is sick, as are two people from a *National Outdoor Leader-ship School (NOLS)* group. Cliff made a flyby and heard that things are improving. I heard from the Vancouver team and they said the Koreans may have had an avalanche problem. Later, the Koreans reported that they were OK, and Vancouver says that they were OK.

Hans flew in. He is a friend of Hans Zogg in Switzerland, who sent his yearly regards, and I sent mine back. We climbed in Mexico together: Hans, Norm Benton, Al and I. Later, a German party flew in, I know Karl from Garmisch. Also *SUWA* flew out. *Garmisch* came down and they gave me a hand warmer present. A *Genet* party made a carry. I helped them with handling ice axes. Genet arrived late tonight. I called Lady Sunflower (one of my radio neighbors out there somewhere) and told her good-bye.

July 10.   I flew out with Cliff and said good-bye on the radio to people out there. I talked to Jeff on my way out.

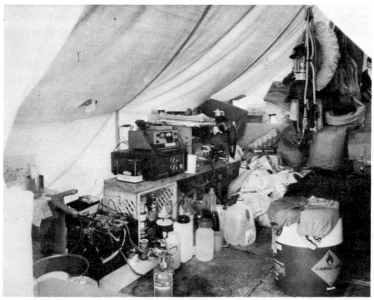

Frances' home on the Kahiltna Glacier, sharing space with food, bedding, rescue gear, radio, weather equipment, etc.

Chapter Five — 1980

Peter Habeler to try
the Wickersham Wall

May 27. Arrived in the afternoon. The weather is getting
marginal. Tom flew me in. He has run the Iditarod several years
and used to be an administrator for medical labs, hospitals,
etc., but he didn't like the stress and pressure.

May 28. Cliff called. Mike Covington called from 15000
feet on the West Rib. *Mountain Trip Traverse* called from 17300
feet. A German couple was last seen on top between 6:00 and
7:00 p.m. yesterday and they have not returned. Mike Donahue,
on the West Buttress, called from 17000 feet. About twenty
climbers are there and they have several problems: 1) the
German couple has not returned, 2) one in a party of three has
altitude sickness, 3) one in another party has frozen feet. I talked
to Cliff, then to Mike Donahue again, and advised all people
with problems to get down the Mountain. I asked if more help
was needed, and advised where help was available. Mike tried
to call but could not maintain contact.

Water Buffalo called from 7300 feet. They had been on the
Cassin; one member had fallen and had injured his leg. They
will bring him to Base Camp. Hans Brunner with the Swiss
group arrived from the Mountain and brought a yearly hello
from Hans Zogg in Switzerland, who used to climb with us in
Seattle. I received a call from Rick Davis at 15000 feet. Very
poor transmission. Only Mike Donahue and Herman Wolfe
stayed at 17000 feet in case the German couple came down.
At 15000 feet there is one person with cerebral edema, one with
frozen feet, and one with frostbite. I advised everyone to get
lower for possible assistance. The radio calls from Mike
Donahue are getting fainter.

May 29. Lowell Thomas, Jr. flew by and tried to land. I
talked to him on the radio at 12000 feet. He can't get down.
I talked to Roy Davis at Montana Creek; he is excellent with
communications. I also talked to Mike Covington at 15000 feet
on the West Rib. He will go to 16500 feet today, return to 15000

feet, and then move camp to 16500 feet tomorrow. The party is OK. Dave Parker (four in party) called from 15000 feet. The person with frostbite says he can't move, but I advised him to get down to 14000 feet. Mike Donahue and Herman Wolfe are now down to 14000 feet. Still no sign of the German couple. I talked to Hans Brunner. The German couple took a silver tent fly with them on the summit ascent from their last camp. They were wearing white bunny boots, red parkas and blue pants. The Germans wanted to stay on top and enjoy view. They lost a pack about 1000 feet down the Mountain. Later, a terrible wind came up. Climbers saw that the pack was not on the route down, which is difficult to find in a storm.

I talked to Cliff and advised of conditions on the Mountain. An Air Force rescue plane is overhead. I talked to them and gave a description of the parties on the Mountain. They will circle for a couple of hours. The *Kyota* party (two) took off (Channel 1 and 2). The Air Force wants Cliff to call collect to the Rescue Coordination Center at Elmendorf regarding rescue capability in Talkeetna for fixed wing aircraft and helicopters. I called Cliff and got a description of the plane overhead: C130, call sign KING 31, tail #95831. They were on a rescue training flight to sight the German couple on the Mountain.

I have contact with Cliff on HF, with the C130 on CB and HF, and with Elmendorf through Cliff. The C130 is now talking to climbing parties, who are in a bad area for reception, and to Base Camp. The cerebral edema case and the frozen feet case are not good. The C130 requested information on equipment and clothing of the German couple. I have contact with Roy Davies about the weather. Complete overcast by tonight. A helicopter has been requested out of Talkeetna. Weather is variable—flying difficult. Jim Opgenet is pilot for AOVA Co. in Talkeetna. He knows the area well. The C130 left the area. The *Water Buffalo* party arrived in Base with the leg injury victim. Lowell Thomas and Tom are here as local fog has grounded them. I gave Tom lunch. Doug was in and took off in a fog bank.

Later, the fog cleared. Flights started again as about twenty-nine people were waiting to fly off the Mountain. I talked to Mike Covington at 15000 feet. He will move day after tomorrow as weather is starting to move in again. He will look for the Germans. K-2 Flying Service has taken all their clients out and has only some gear left to fly out.

The German, from the *Genet* party led by Tim from Australia, came in. He was very upset about the missing Germans. I asked his name and it sounded as if it was from the Mideast. He had a Mideast accent and looked like he came from there. He was nearly hysterical, begged to get out, swore at his climbing party, and blamed everything and everybody for the German problem. He said his nerves were shot and he would pay for his own separate flight out. I talked to Cliff and arranged for him to go with no gear with the Hudson Flying Service when Jay and Tom fly in. I talked to Jay and Tom and introduced them to Mesib Suleki. Suleki started ranting and raving again. They took him out. Later I learned that Suleki was a great problem on the Mountain. He was an Iranian who left Iran about the time of the Shah and had just gotten his German citizenship the day before he left on this climb. He was very erratic and excitable. Later, Sunny was mad because Suleki was Lowell Thomas' passenger. Suleki was taken out by Hudson Air Service due to imminent danger of Suleki here to himself, to others or to property, by him wandering off, or any combination of these things. Bush pilots have short tempers.

I received the newspaper from you and thank you. I also received a letter from a young man who was staying in my cabin. He had gotten a job in Haines. And I received a letter from the NPS with instructions for Mike Covington. Mike Covington called and I relayed the contents of the letter from the NPS. Two flew in to do the southwest face of McKinley. They had purchased their tent from 'Dale Bard. They are from Los Angeles. Two flew in to do the Cassin: Mike Helms and Bob Kandiko. Five Japanese from Tokyo arrived; they are sponsored by Japanese Railroads and are employees of Japan Railways. Nine from *RMI* (Seattle) arrived for a training trip and possible climb of the West Ridge of Hunter.

The *Bronze Carabiners* (two) arrived. They had spent the night at 19000 feet in a hole in the ice while the storm moved. They are lucky to have survived. The Germans were found about 300 feet above where they had been. With wind velocities such as the ones here on the Mountain you can not stand, crawl, or see. The *Haas-Swiss-Gorman* group (three), which has been here at Base, left for the southeast fork of Foraker. Ten from *Mountain Trip* are going to do a traverse over the Mountain. A Japanese group came over—they speak no English and are going to try the northeast ridge, which is pure suicide. I tried to talk to them, but planes are coming and going all the time while the weather lasts, plus the radio is going, so I made arrangements with the Japanese to talk with them at 9:00 p.m.

Tokyo Unryokai called. Mike Covington called; he had gone to 19500 feet. Tomorrow he will try for the summit or move to 18000 feet. He didn't see the bodies of the German couple. The Japanese team left without communication. They said they will start climbing in two days. If they survive it will be a miracle. Mike Covington called. Winds last night and now are 150 miles per hour and are blowing the radio waves around. Mike may not be able to go to the summit at all. Nick needs crampons: SMC, extra large (relayed through Rose Hill). I talked to Ollie and reordered the crampons. Tried to reach *Kyoto*. Mike Covington called from 16500 feet; he will wait there until Thursday and then either go up or come down. Visibility is three inches. I tried to call *Hosaki* on Foraker. The Austrian party is not OK at 17000 feet; one member is sick. Three American climbers are there and want to try to summit tomorrow. K-2 landed.

Peter Habeler, a famous Austrian climber who climbed Everest without oxygen, and Michl Meirer, also from Austria, are going to try Wickersham Wall, or do something else. *Pickl and Winfried*, from Nuremberg, flew out. A member of their group was evacuated with cerebral edema several days ago by helicopter, along with the victim of frozen feet. Strobel, Gunter and Platzer remain. *Tokyo Unryokai* members are OK and report that *Kyoto* is OK. The Austrian party called; four are at 10000 feet, one has pulmonary edema, and they will bring the ill person to Base Camp tomorrow. Others at 17000 feet will try for the summit tomorrow.

June 4.   Robert Cedargreen came down with Mike Graeber. Robert is to fly out; Mike plans to solo the West Buttress. Eric Reynolds is to fly out, and Eric Dirksen and Bob Hastington are to ski out 40 miles to Petersville. Joy and Tom flew in *Windsinger* (five) to do the West Buttress. They'll be on Channel 1-40. The Austrian team of four came down the Mountain to fly out with Hudson; they are Buckner, Lucer, Viser and Hans, who has pulmonary edema, but is in pretty good shape here. Mike Covington is at 19400 feet. It's foggy there. *Mountain Travel Seminar* (seven) flew in with Gary Bocarde, the leader. Doug brought in four Germans from Munich to do a traverse. Mike Covington is on the summit. Three people have seen the bodies of the German climbers. Mike can not bring down the bodies as he has some tired people.

Lowell Thomas came in with a German photographer. They left a plane door here so the photographer could take pictures. Doug flew in Brian Larson (from New Zealand) to do a solo climb of the Cassin. (No one this year has been able to climb Cassin.) Lowell Thomas came in again to change film, and came back later to pick up the door. *Tokyo Unryokai* called. I received a message from *Mountain Trip Traverse* that Roy Turmell is to go out. *Mountain Trip Seminar* is not strong enough. Roy Turmell is in Base Camp with Nick Parker and Wolfgang, as Roy decided to fly out. I talked to both *Mountain Trip Traverse* and *Mountain Travel Seminar* earlier due to this change in groups. *Mountain Trip Traverse* called and will try to contact Gary Bocarde of *Mountain Travel Seminar* tonight at 9:00 p.m. and will relay if communication is bad.

WCK2: Stephen Lake wants Cliff to fly out a couple of people. Talkeetna could not copy. I relayed to Talkeetna. K-2 Aviation flew in with seven from *Anchorage Community College*. Gunner is their leader. Jay flew in with *RMI*. A call came in from 17000 feet about a sick climber. They could not copy me, so I do not know the name of the party. They speak with a slight accent—not Japanese. *Mountain Trip Traverse* and *Mountain Travel Seminar* (Gary Bocarde) called. Gary also tried to contact 17000 feet. I monitored the radio till 10:30 p.m., and periodically made calls to 17000 feet. They are constantly calling and the radio is fading. They probably have a malfunctioning set, or the transmitter button is in or the squelch button is turned on too much.

June 6. Ollie called at 7:00 a.m.; the weather is not good in Talkeetna. At 10:00 Doug came in with seven from Colorado. *Haas-Swiss-Gorman* flew out. The *Two High Band* called from 14000 feet; everything is OK. There are twelve people in the area. Doug flew up to 12000 feet to look at the trouble at 17000 feet. No oxygen; he came down from about 12000 feet. There were very high turbulent winds; he is now having ear trouble. The *Colorado Cuties* (six girls plus one man) are coming in with Doug to do the West Buttress. I talked to Bocarde and to Verne of *Mountain Trip Traverse*. Simo left tent poles for George of *RMI* and he will send sleds down the hill. *Kanda* is back from nearly 17000 feet. He reported terrible winds and that there are two Japanese at 10000 feet, four or five parties at 12000 feet, five or six parties at 14000 feet, seven or eight on the West Rib, and one solo around 12000 feet. Mike Covington walked in. I talked to Mike. There's a crevasse near the bodies of the Germans that could be used for possible burial; otherwise a special team will be needed to go up and recover them. They would be impossible to recover in the storm. Someone will have to call the family. Mike said his group had to lie flat in self arrest in many places. Another time the wind blew his sled and he almost lost his hand. When he last saw the Austrians, they looked weak and sick; they had heavy parkas, but their tents were in the open—wrong location.

June 7. In the all-women-plus-one-man team, one has a bladder infection and another has strep throat. They need prescriptions filled. I talked to Mike Covington some more. The three Americans in the area of the Austrians were *Big Mac*. He also saw three going down, which was probably a Japanese team on the West Buttress. Mike Covington's party, *Big Mac* and the Austrians will come together at 19300 feet. Covington talked to the Americans mostly. Communications are terrible: nothing on HF, but I can hear Talkeetna. The only CB communication is with the Japanese CB set in this immediate area. Doug came in with another two women. I gave him the prescription and a grocery list for two other climbers. Doug flew in the *Outlaws* (two) to do the West Buttress or the West Rib. *Emmental* came down. Marty saw the Austrian party start down. There are also three Germans *(Nuremburg)* up there. The *Wednesday Night Sourdoughs* (five) are going to 17000 feet. Marty also saw six from Boulder, Colorado. The *Kenya 80* group (three) came in, and *Kanda* went out. I talked with the Japanese quite a bit. The *Tristate* party (two) came in. Jack was here last year; I'm always running into people I've met before. The *Two High Band* called from 16000 feet; they saw the German and Austrian teams coming down. The Austrians told them that the Japanese may be higher. Mike Covington's group went out and the *Wolfgang-Austrian* group (four) came in. Dave Bard and McQuery came back after an unsuccessful try on the West Buttress of Mt. Hunter. A German party (three) is back. They lost their tents, so are staying in my red tent. Jay came in and couldn't take off because of the fog, so he stayed in the red tent with the Germans. I tried to reach Cliff to let him know that Jay is here. Cliff was overhead looking for Jay and saw the airplane so everything is OK.

June 8.   Talked to Cliff. Ordered new tent poles from Cathy who is running Genet's outfit. Jay flew out with the other Swiss team. I received a call from K-2 Aviation. Very bad communication. A plane is upside down on the Tokositna Glacier at 8000 feet. Four people including the pilot were on board, but no one was hurt. They requested a call to Hudson Air Service. I called Talkeetna but got no answer. I made an urgent call to Hayes River, and got Talkeetna. Ollie called back. Cliff tried to broadcast blind to K-2. Doug called from Kichatna Spires. I talked to the Germans. Tom flew in and out. The *Scottish-American* group (two) is here. They have no radio and want to try some new routes on Foraker, McKinley, and Hunter. Tom called from over One Shot Pass. I can barely copy Cliff talking to someone. Jay is talking to Cliff, who is over the Tokositna and will land shortly.

I hear Jay and Cliff. Jay came in, took two climbers to the Buckskin Glacier near Moose's Tooth. *Big Mac* (three) came down; two are from Wenatchee, one is from Tacoma. *Three Blind Geeks* called from 14000 feet; there are about six people in the area. The *Two High Band* is at Denali Pass on their way up. Doug took *Big Mac* out. The *Two High Band* passed the bodies of the two Germans at 19300 feet. Two Austrians came in. One Austrian was here, which made a total of thirteen in that party, not twelve as records had indicated. Cliff is coming in and talking to *Windsinger* at 14000 feet and going to 16000 feet. Beautiful weather. Gary Bocarde called; he said he saw five descending Crosson, and also saw tracks on the southeast ridge of Foraker (Japanese). It looks like tracks started up the northeast ridge, but he never saw the Japanese after their camp below the ridge. The *Two High Band* was at 17000 feet and may be down to 14000 feet. Jay came in and took the last Austrian team out. The *Banks* team (five) are in from the Crosson-Foraker traverse. They saw the Japanese (five). I called Cliff; Jay, coming through One Shot Pass, relayed the message to Doug that one of the *Banks* groups wants to go out.

June 9.   Kelly Holland was in and out to bring in four from *McGill*. One member of *Kenya 80*, Mark Savage, came back. He couldn't stand the tremendous size of the glacier and mountains. He has climbed Mt. Kenya a lot and also Kilimanjaro. There was one person last year, I think from California, who also couldn't stand the vastness of it here and had to leave.

Radio test with *McGill*. Mike Graeber came down; he did

McKinley solo in 4-5 days. He reported that *Mountain Trip Traverse* is at 11000 feet, *RMI* is at 12600 feet, the *Colorado Cuties* are at 11000 feet, *Swissmiss* is at 12500 feet. *Knittell* (four) (Karl and Anne's friend) are very strong; they put two on the summit today and two on the summit last night. The *Wednesday Night Sourdoughs* (five) are at 17000 feet and coming down. Gary Bocarde called; he has two climbers that want to leave and will be here in several hours. A C130 flew overhead. The *Outlaws* are at 9500 feet and are going to switch from the West Buttress to the West Rib. They saw two Japanese go to Cassin Ridge. This year, no one has climbed the Cassin and only Mike Covington and *Knittell* have done the West Rib.

19V (Lowell Thomas) flew in and brought cauliflower, cabbage, broccoli, yogurt, potatoes, apple juice, fruit cocktail, canned peaches and several Red Delicious apples (not my favorite). *Mountain Trip Traverse* is at 13000 feet, and will go to 14200 feet tomorrow. Gary Bocarde is over by Crosson and plans to go to 9000 feet tonight. Cliff flew in and took out two from Gary's party. Cliff brought chicken, bread, and garlic powder. Lowell Thomas came in with Brian Okonek and Dianne from Genet's group. I met Dianne, who was on tour with National Park Service, and I've known Brian for years. Conditions are clouding up.

June 10. I talked to Cliff and asked him to call Anne "collect" to let her know that *Knittell* was probably coming down, and also to ask about getting a gut attachment for my violin. The attachment goes between the tail piece and peg, which broke and caused a crack. I told him to contact David Crawford, as he would know what I need.

Got a message from Roy Davies and Roger from NPS for Brian. A contract is going to be worked out to bring the bodies down. The parents wish the bodies to be brought down. I advised that Brian was out on the glacier in a seminar and I couldn't go out alone unroped, but would relay the message. Brian radioed to Roy, who relayed to Doug and Roger (NPS) that he would need 600 feet of rope for a fixed line, six pickets and twelve carabiners.

June 11. Brian came over; Marty Brenner in his party has symptoms of stroke. His left leg and arm show weakness, loss of mobility at times. I got in touch with Roy Davies, who got in touch with Marge of Talkeetna Medics, to get the procedure to follow to administer medical assistance in Base Camp. Marge said the patient needs to be evacuated to a hospital, but it's impossible to evacuate in a whiteout. Also, he needs oxygen, which we don't have. Marty must be kept quiet and warm and in a prone position with shoulder and feet elevated. We also need to get his pulse, temperature, and vitals. Marty is in his early 40s and is a physicist. He has a son on the climb, and has an unusual father-son relationship according to the leader, Brian, and assistant leader, Dianne. Vitals: temperature 98.6 (usually high 97s), pulse 92 (usually 66-68), respiration 21/min., runs two to four miles per day.

Marge, Talkeetna Medics, told Roy that we needed to get his blood pressure. Brian is an EMT but he couldn't remember the procedure to get the systolic blood pressure and there is no blood pressure kit here. Also, no stethoscope. The procedure: using a vein in the wrist, count beats per minute for one full minute. His systolic pressure is 88 (normal pressure 115/72). Diagnosis: symptoms indicate heart attack. Procedure: Let him suck on a wet cloth to moisten the lips, but give no great amount of liquid and no solids. It seems that he has had the problem for a couple of days, which indicates that it could be either a stroke or a heart attack. I called Roy to get a procedure for long-range care in case of bad weather here. Procedure: Play it by ear, i.e. give light broth, but no solids.

Cathy, who is running Genet's outfit, called from Talkeetna about the heart patient being the first person out. Cathy called again about the heart patient: Dr. Mills in Anchorage has been contacted. He advised food and lots of H2-O. He also asked if the patient had any previous medical history (no), and if he takes any medication (no). He also asked if he had any symptoms of pulmonary edema (no). I checked with Roy about the apparently conflicting procedure given by the Talkeetna Medics. They said that the 'food' was fluid, so the problem is solved. Scott Emery, M.D., neurologist, Elmendorf Air force Hospital with privilege at Providence, came in. Emery examined Marty but could not say for sure what is wrong without hospital and clinic facilities. He thinks it is probably a slight stroke, but it may be a danger signal of something else. The patient definitely needs to get out.

Now we have two EMTs here, a stethoscope, a psychiatrist and an anesthetist. I called Roy and advised Dr. Emery had examined Marty, that the condition is not critical, but that he needs medical attention and should get off the Mountain as soon as possible. It probably was caused by a sloughing off of tissue in the artery, which starts at age fifteen, but it should be investigated further.

RMI is at 14000 feet; three are coming down to bring one that has to go out. John Svenson, from Gary's group, will stay for the next *Mountain Trip* group to come in. *Mountain Trip Traverse* is at 13000 feet. Eason and Charlie Hoffman are at 17000 feet. *Munich* (four) is at 17000 feet, and there may be a solo climber in area. Robert Milne and Brian Sprunt (Scotland) are back from Hunter; they bivouacked in a storm on the buttress and were stormed off. There is an emergency at 14000 feet. *Mountain Trip* is at 14000 feet. I talked to Verne, who said someone is injured and needs a helicopter evacuation.

June 12. Three Czechs are in trouble at 19000 feet, near Archdeacon's Tower. Peter descended to 14000 feet to bring word. I called Talkeetna. Then I talked to *Mountain Trip* and advised them of the impossibility of rescue at that altitude. Doug is on the way in to get the heart/stroke patient and the other respiratory problem. Two injured climbers are at Denali Pass; one EMT, as well as seven others are going to Denali Pass. I talked to others at 17200 feet approaching Denali Pass. Two Americans and one German are there and other parties are going to help. Peter Habeler, at 14000 feet noted the lone figure, which he had seen on the summit from below. He had down-climbed the Messner Couloir. Doug tried to do a flyby up to 17000 feet. *Outlaw* (two) is on the West Buttress and has not seen the Japanese parties. Gary came out with the edema and respiratory patients. *Hosaki* (three) came out. Kenny flew in with three. Earlier, Lowell Thomas took out two sick people. The two people are down from 18000 feet to 17200 feet. They are Germans: (1) 38, 170 lbs., respiration shallow, cyanotic, pulse 92, pupils equal, eyes glassy, skin dry, can not hold fluids or solids; (2) 38, approximately 190 lbs., joints swollen (indicates edema), appears in state of shock, extreme fatigue, despondent, but can walk. Michl Meirer is down to 17200 feet; he was out for two nights and days and has no food. It seems impossible to bring one of the injured men down, but I advised that the only way he can live is to bring him down. One of injured climbers has a broken pelvis, which extends to the spine, and internal bleeding.

Now, two Czechs are at 18000 feet (instead of Americans or Germans). The Army has choppers available on thirty-minutes notice. The party of the injured climbers is Czech; they came up the Muldrow to 18000 feet. I talked to KES7604 (Roy). A rescue is on the way. Col. Whittaker will make the decisions on the rescue. Five or seven people are up there in the area to help. I hear that NPS 6832995 is the aircraft headed for the site. A C130 is to come in one hour from Anchorage, and Chinooks in four hours from Fairbanks. Fort Wainwright wants to know the type of communication available on the Mountain. Roy said they need to know the weather, the exact position of the party, whether they have CBs at 18000 feet, and what type of batteries they have (a CB takes eight AA penlight batteries). There is a CB at 17000 feet and one at 18000 feet. Weather: blue skies, a few fluffy clouds, winds 0, temperature 35 degrees Fahrenheit. One patient is critical: he cannot take fluids, vomited blood, refuses intake, and his legs are numb from the pelvis down.

I advised that we have synchronized our watches on the Mountain to save batteries by reporting at intervals. Roy called; he advised that the C130 radio must go amplitude modulation (AM), not single side band (SSB). I advised *Mountain Trip* at 17000 feet. Fort Wainwright is loading up now; if they can get batteries, they will, but will not delay the mission. I advised other parties to stay off the air when the C130 is here unless the C130 requests information. A radio transmission from 17000 feet to 18000 feet, back to 17000 feet and then to Base Camp: They are marking out a landing site for the helicopter at 18000 feet. The patient's condition is getting more serious. The C130 is due in 40 minutes, three hours before the Chinooks arrive. It will rendezvous in Talkeetna to pick up a medic. Another call from 17000 feet to 18000 feet, back to 17000 feet and to Kahiltna Base: there is no wind at 17000 feet; it is clear at 18000 feet with winds at 15 knots, 20-25 degrees Fahrenheit. At 18000 feet, one victim is critical, the other is delirious. One party showed up about an hour ago, all Czechs. Five others, Americans and Germans are assisting. At 17000 feet there are sixteen to twenty people preparing to send food up.

Miyazaki (four), on the West Buttress is on the Japanese Channel, 19. Bill Wilson, from the *Eason Expedition*, is talking at 17000 feet. They report that the condition of the patient is unchanged, and inquire about dropping a litter with batteries. The chopper probably will drop the batteries. Roy asked NPS if they knew the size of the party that came up the Muldrow.

There were four Czechs in the party, according to NPS. One New Zealand solo climber came in, got to 15800 feet, and went out later with Tom. He reported that the ten-man Czech party should be at 18000 feet on the South Buttress; but two are at their base at 11700 feet. One Czech at 11700 feet speaks English and Czech. One Englishman at 18000 feet speaks Czech and English. The C130 is off SSB and on AM. I advised the Air Force that there were four people in the Czech party. They read 5x5 (loud and clear) and reported they are five miles out and coming in. I talked to the C130 to advise of conditions and situations: low on batteries, condition of patient, Kahiltna Base on standby. The C130 communicated directly with 18000 feet. It is going to try to drop medical supplies and blankets at Denali for the patients. KES7604 says the helio C130 will be here in one hour.

The Chinooks are leaving Talkeetna and should be here at 9:00 p.m. A helicopter passed by; I took pictures with the Leica. The C130 advised the Chinook to burn off gas to gain altitude and also to make a couple of dry runs and then be in to pick up the patients. At approximately 10:00 p.m. the C130 advised that the patients were on board and two choppers passed overhead (the rescue Chinook and a larger black-cover chopper. The C130 advised that the rescued climbers are secured and "Thanks Kahiltna Base and KES7604 (Roy)." Weather closed in. The radio contact at 18000 feet was John Morris of *Windsinger,* an ex-Marine. At 17000 feet, the radio contact was Bill Wilson of *Eason* , a communications specialist from Vietnam. At 7300 feet, Kahiltna Base, radio contact was Frances Randall. KES7604, Roy Davies, ex- communications, retired. Thanks, received letters and papers and flower. Your letter of June 12, 1980, saying "no seismic activity" was surely a warning for the **BIG BANG** on June 13, 1980 (St. Helen's).

June 13. 5:50 a.m. Charged batteries. I tested radios with *Donauworth.* Carlos of the *Genet* party brought Marty Brenner's gear down. I tested radios with *Cascade* and *Butterfly. Water Buffalo* made the Cassin; they are coming down. Later, Doug brought in Peter Carter from the Ruth Glacier; he may join friends. At 14000 feet, *Three Blind Geeks* advise that everyone is descending today or tomorrow. Twenty or thirty people are in the area. *Mountain Trip Traverse* and *Knittell* are at 16200 feet. A party of Germans moved to 18000 feet. Rob Milne and friend left. *Munich Expedition* is on the Traverse.

One member of *Windsinger* made the summit yesterday. *Munich* and the rest of *Windsinger* plan to go up tomorrow. Doug Bilman of *Three Blind Geeks* (the radio contact at 14000 feet) is on the way down. *Butterfly*, at 7300 feet is going to 9000 feet.

June 14. *Knittell* (four) and *Three Blind Geeks* are waiting for Hudson. The *RMI-Hunter* group (nine) that did Hunter are here for Doug. I talked to Doug (medic) of *Three Blind Geeks*. He confirmed that two Americans and Michl Meirer were at 18000 feet, and that Peter Habeler was at the top when he saw two Czechs in the area of Archdeacon's Tower. They could hardly move and had been there two or three days. He brought them to Denali Pass. Three stayed at Denali Pass while Peter took off down the Messner Couloir because he knew there was a radio at 14000 feet. *Three Blind Geeks* saw a third Czech; he had an ankle injury, wouldn't let anyone touch him and took off later. They suspect that he had a sprained ankle at least, and was not in good shape. No one has seen the fourth member. *Water Buffalo* (two) is coming down with Norma Jean of *Colorado Cuties*. She has severe frostbite of the feet. *Infinite Odyssey* (nine), on the West Buttress, is on Channel 19. They tried to walk up the glacier, got to Dutch Creek, which was very high, had difficulties, and walked back to Cache Creek. Bill walked back to Peters Fork to phone. They are now flying into Kahiltna Base to start their traverse.

I talked to Cliff: of the two Czechs that were evacuated, one is stable and the other is walking around. Someone needs an ice saw. No ice saw for sale here. *Outlaw* is at 14000 feet and can see the top. *Twin Cities*, West Rib, is on Channel 19. *RMI-Traverse* is at 16500 feet. Bob Wilson is coming down with *Mountain Trip*. Two Japanese went to 17000 feet. The *Colorado Cuties* went to 17000 feet, then back to 14000 feet. Peter Habeler and Michl Meirer are going up. *Swissmiss* is on the West Rib now, from the West Buttress, at 16400 feet.

June 15. Cliff called and advised me to check the oil in the generator and to get hydrometer readings on the battery: Upper Left, 1125 (needs water); Upper Right, 1150; Center Left, 1200; Center Right, 1200; Lower Left, 1200; Lower Right, 1200. *Windsinger* is at 17000 feet, going down; they reached the top. Four of *Munich* party are there. *Mountain Trip Traverse* is at 16200 feet. Michael Bradley is down from *Mountain Trip Traverse*. Take stuff to Jim Hale or have Cliff keep. *Infinite*

Odyssey is going on a crevasse-rescue practice over by Hunter. *Tristate* (two), at 14000 feet, asked if they have a message from *Outlaw*—none. The ten Czechs are in; they made the summit. Cliff ordered things for the Czechs: Orolin, Fiala, Petrik, Haak, Nevemann, Bakos, Weinfeller, Kovaa, Frantisek, Johnson. I talked with Dave Johnson, who is an Englishman married to a Czech and they live in Czechoslovakia. He advised of an unexplainable incident on their route, which was a new route on the South Buttress: on Cassin Ridge at 10500 feet are three pair of skis; were there on May 27 and were still there on June 15.

Cliff called: The Czechs have a radio they are to give to the Italians to use on Channel A (Channel 19). *Butterfly* at 8300 feet is OK. *Swissmiss* at 19000 feet will go to the summit tomorrow. *Mountain Trip Traverse* is at 17200 feet and will go to the summit day after tomorrow. *RMI* is at 17200 feet; they will summit tomorrow. Both parties have radios. The Italians are in: Friuli, C. Floreanini, F. Cofetti, C. DeCrignts, L. DeCrignts, L. Querini, F. DeSanciis, Rainis. All but three Czechs got out. The Italians are very excitable—they are dressed in red like an Olympic Ski team. They started out in the wrong direction, towards Foraker, but finally asked for direction. I tried to start the generator; it started and then stopped like it was out of gas, or possibly had water or foreign material in the gas.

June 16. The generator still will not work; I called Roy. Roy relayed to Talkeetna and requested someone to bring up HEAT. *RMI* and *Mountain Trip Traverse* have a CB on Channel 19. *Bottoms UP* (three) is on the West Buttress. *USA* (Seattle) is Charles Gary, Paul Hickenbottom. Three Czechs went out. Jay forgot the HEAT. *RMI* is on the summit; Mountain Trip will go tomorrow. Four Germans headed toward Harper. I called Ollie about the generator, the HEAT, pliers, screw drivers, and tools to take out the spark plug. Jay came in and out. Two Czechs went out. Jay's girl friend is here; he also brought the next two of the Seattle party to do the West Rib. Jay came in with the rest of the *Hoofers*. He investigated the generator; HEAT did not help. Jay says to take off one bolt and clean the generator; he removed a spark plug, the one here is too big. Jay took the spark plug which was badly eroded. The *Outlaws* (two) called that they and *Tristate* will be down tomorrow. I contacted Doug. Vernon of *Mountain Trip Traverse* gave me a message to relay to Nancy, but I couldn't copy.

Peter Habeler and Michl Meirer are back. *Mountain Trip Traverse* tried to call again, but reception is still bad. Jay took off with his girl friend. He would not take Peter or Michl because he said he had other passengers to pick up. Also, he let the last of the Czechs (two) sit hours waiting, when he could have gotten in in good weather. *Windsinger* (five) was back at the bottom of the hill when Jay took off. Later, John Svenson of *Mountain Trip Traverse* and *Glacier Slugs* (one) and Peter and Michl and I talked about climbing, music and travel agencies. Peter does not underestimate Mt. McKinley and stresses the need to dig in at the first sign of change in the weather. An Italian came back; he strained a muscle in his leg; I gave him food, water, and a tent to stay in.

June 17.   I need a spark plug, a back-up battery and the generator taken out if the spark plug does not work. Peter and Michl can work on the generator. Jay came in, and brought a spark plug. The generator still doesn't work. Jay took Peter and Michl (they are K-2 passengers) plus the Italian out. I took some pictures. *Swissmiss* is at Archdeacon's Tower. *Windsinger* requested that I call Cliff because of the weather. Two will lose $200 if they don't get on their super-saver plane fare. I talked to Cliff and it's OK with him if a switch is made in flight arrangements so that either pilot takes two of Hudson's clients and one of Doug's with a badly ulcerated tooth. *RMI* is at 17000 feet, *Mountain Trip Traverse, Kyoto,* the Austrian party and the *Colorado Cuties* also are there. Cliff called. NPS to *RMI:* one Czech died in the tent at 16000 feet; the other was evacuated. NPS requested *RMI* to drag out the contents of the tent to 15000 feet for easier helicopter evacuation. Every member has been or will be evacuated by helicopter. The Italians want to know if their injured member made it back to Base. The *Tokyo* group on the Cassin is at 13000 feet or 14000 feet and advised I need to contact *Kyoto at 17000 feet. Tricities* is back.

June 18.   I tried to contact parties on the Mountain to get hold of *Mountain Trip Traverse.* Cliff called and advised that either *Mountain Trip Traverse* or *RMI* will bring the Czech tent down. I hear Unalakleet on HF. *Swissmiss* was on the summit last night. I talked to Scott about Mike's tooth. The *Outlaws* have erythromycin. I also talked to *Mountain Trip* and *Glacier Slugs* about the Czech problem on the Harper Glacier. They confirmed that Jay was on the glacier with his girl friend until 9:00 or 10:00 p.m. Mike's tooth, the third from rear on top right, was ulcerated when he was in the seventh grade and they capped it. He does not recall an incision.

The generator was fixed yesterday by the *Outlaws*. Mike, with the bad tooth, is a mechanic. He drained the water out of the tank and cleaned the filter in the carburetor. I talked to Bob Holmes of *Windsinger* about seeing Mr. Kim in Anchorage if they lose their Super-Saver. They (*Windsinger*) were at the bottom of the hill when Jay took off with his girl friend. I relayed a message to Doug for Scott of *Outlaws*: call his wife. We discussed the medical problem (Mike's ulcerated tooth): no dentist in Talkeetna, medics do not know answer. Dr. Lee Podal here (of *Tristate*) wanted a second opinion. We will start administering erythromycin. Mike experienced pain at 17000 feet, which did not respond to Demerol; the swelling is now up to eye and the condition is worse today. I relayed a message for John Morris of *Windsinger* (radio contact man and ex-marine) to call his wife about the possibility of them not making their flight due to weather.

I advised Cliff that I had talked to *Mountain Trip* and *Glacier Slugs* about the Czech problem; all four have been accounted for. A third member was rescued at 15000 feet or 16000 feet; the fourth is dead and will be evacuated. (All members were flown off by helicopter above 15000 feet). The *Hoofers* are at 7600 feet; I heard another party toward northeast fork and advised that if they heard *Mountain Trip* or *RMI* to contact Kahiltna Base. We synchronized watches.

Cliff called and I relayed the message to call David Sharpe's *(Windsinger)* folks. *RMI* is at 17000 feet; I relayed the information about the Czech in the tent at 16000 to be brought, with the contents intact, down to 15000 feet for helicopter pick-up. Brian Okonek, with the *Genet* party, is going to bring the German bodies back to 14000 feet. *Mountain Trip Traverse, Kyoto,* and *Granger Banks* are at 17000 feet. The Germans of Munich have started down the traverse. *Swissmiss* will come down today. *RMI* to go up on first clear day. Lowell Thomas is overhead, and advised that the *Genet* group is below 17000 feet. I advised that Marty Brenner's bag is here. Lowell Thomas told the *Genet* group that another low pressure system is moving in across the Aleutians. Lowell Thomas told Brian that he is at 14000 feet and it seems to be OK there. Gunnar and Brian are going to 17000 feet. Lowell Thomas is going to climb higher. I got the news about St. Helens.

RMI is going down the Harper. I relayed to NPS that they will be there approximately 5:00 p.m. and will try to get to the Muldrow tonight. *Mountain Trip Traverse* asked me to relay a message to Nancy. I tried to get a German telegram again. I talked to *Mountain Trip Traverse* about the Czechs. If *RMI* cannot pick them up, then *Mountain Trip Traverse* and *Glacier Slugs* will do it. I relayed the message to Nancy, and also got the Germans, *Munich*, scheduled to send out. *Tokyo Unryokai* called. Also *Lady Sunflower*. I briefly heard 3167 Pribilof trying to contact Rev. Nimonsky in Sitka. Finally, I tried to relay: I called Cliff but he couldn't locate such a Rev. in Sitka. Also, I sent a message for Daniel *(Windsinger)* to his parents.

June 20.   Recharged the battery. *Hoofers* (four) and USA are at 8500 feet and all OK; they cannot see anyone climbing down. Cliff called—there's a possibility of flying tomorrow.

June 21.   *Swissmiss* and *Butterfly* are here. There has been a split in *Butterfly*. Tom is going back up. Father Tim is going to Anchorage. Three Catholic priests are here. I talked to Rose Hill to relay to Cliff and advise him to call before taking off as wind is changing from local northeast to general high and local west and southwest. *Mountain Trip Traverse* at 18000 feet is OK; *Kyoto* is OK; *Colorado Cuties* are OK; *USA* (three) is OK. One person of the *McCartney-Roberts* group is sick on the Mountain: no edema. (Transmission by clicks from transmitter button). I switched to Channel 1, then back to 19. I called Cliff about the sick person on the Mountain; communication with 18000 feet is very poor. I can only hear that there is a possible problem with one person. I charged the battery. Mike Helms is at 17200 feet on the West Buttress. Simon McCartney is at 19300 feet on the Cassin with acute mountain sickness. Kandiko is with him.

Mike Helms brought Roberts, who has frostbite, over the top and down the West Buttress to relay a message outside. Helms can get McCartney down to 14000 feet. In an urgent call to contact Cliff by relay to Talkeetna, I tried to get KES7604 and was overheard by a pilot over an island near Kodiak Island. I talked to Mike Helms. There is no radio on the Cassin. *Mountain Trip Traverse* (eight) and the Austrians (three) are at 18000 feet; Gunnar and Helms are at 17000 feet. Helms was using Gunnar's radio. I talked to Ollie. Then I talked to Cliff about the problems at 19300 feet; he cannot make a rescue or drop at that location on the Cassin. *Swissmiss* has one injured member who is also being brought back. Mike Helms called; he has a rescue plan, and he did not see *Kenya 80*, the *Scottish* team, or the *Freaks* below on the Cassin. The Japanese have a radio. Mike has an equipment list for rescue, needs fuel and food, wants to talk to NPS directly. Cliff called and wanted to know if McCartney could stand up. I advised I would ask at 6:00 p.m. I also advised that a group is getting ready to go help. Mike called. *Mountain Trip Traverse* at 18000 feet and Mike Helms is at 17000 feet. Mike Helms advised that:

1) *Mountain Trip Traverse* needs batteries and is willing to assist on the rescue.
2) Must understand gravity.
3) They request a flyover so that Kandiko and McCartney will work to get down.
4) They plan to bring them up over the ridge (about 800 feet) rather than down-climb the Cassin
5) They request a weather report.
6) Weather is clear at 17200 feet, winds calm; at 18000 feet, the winds have died down to 40-50 knots.
7) They need a 6:30 p.m. contact, and then every quarter hour.

Brian, at 14000 feet, says winds are calm, just over top of clouds. NPS requested the list be relayed to them from Mike. Mike, Kahiltna Base, KES7604, NPS: (1) two CB radios, (2) bolt kit with anchors, (3) three hammers, (4) one litter, (5) one winch, (6) six flukes, (7) 1200 feet of cable, (8) one large tent, (9) a first-aid kit, (10) enough fuel and food for sixteen men for five days, (11) smoke bombs. NPS reconfirmed the party to help. Mike says McCartney is in very serious shape and we should try to get him and Kandiko to move up the ridge. NPS advised that Peter Habeler and Michl Meirer are willing to come back to help. NPS wants visibility at 17000 feet and at 18000 feet. They can provide everything but the winch. Mike Helms said that at 17000 feet it is clear, winds are 15-20 knots; at 18000 feet, there are clouds and winds of 35-50 knots. I talked to Roy and advised that *RMI* is still here and not on the Harper Glacier because of the loss of time with the Czech rescue.

Brian is at 14000; also the *Genet* party, *Aspen-Denali* (two), *Kyoto* (two) with Richard Tyrell, *Colorado Cuties* (two); at 17000 feet are *Wolfgang* (three), *McGill* (three). The *Banks Expedition* is in the vicinity of Kahiltna Pass and plans to go out the Peters Glacier to Wonder Lake. Charlie Reed is in Base Camp.

Mountain Trip Traverse called about the weather. McCartney and Kandiko should be at Denali Pass soon. Two groups came in, *Valley-Denali* (six), and *Beglenger* (three) to do the Cassin (these are Swiss and later helped rescue McCartney). *Twin-Cities* is at 12000 feet on the West Rib with no radio (Kurt Mendenhall, Rick Berens).

June 22. Richard Tyrell notified me that one of the *Kyoto* men has had an epileptic seizure. Tyrell ran down to get medical assistance. He had looked at the patient so he could be an eye witness for the medical assistance in Talkeetna. *RMI* has a doctor (eye doctor) with them. I called Cliff; he is standing by for the diagnosis. Simo (E. Simonson, *RMI* leader) said Tony is the MD. The Japanese gave the patient another Valium after quieting him down and putting him in a sleeping bag. The patient is very dehydrated and lacks salt. I talked to Cliff 8:00 a.m.; there is no word from climbing parties above. Apparently the MD decided it was OK to let the patient rest rather than have Cliff come out. Later, Tony decided that the patient should go to the hospital. He does not have a history of epilepsy and may have some brain damage. I finally got hold of KES7604 on the emergency channel (Cliff had turned off his radio and gone to bed). Cliff called from the air and will be here in ten minutes. I notified Tony and *RMI*. Tony is to go along to help in case the patient has another seizure in the airplane. Cliff was in and out with *Kyoto* (two) and Tony.

Tokositna called: the mechanics over there want to leave (they are the ones who dismantled the K-2 airplane that flipped over on landing). Sunny called through KES7604, advised that Tokositna mechanics called at 4:00, 6:00, 8:00. The mechanics are getting low on food and the climbers over there are not very interested in their situation. They are living in the fuselage, which is like an ice box. *RMI* says they have six *RMI* people ready to go, and asked *Swissmiss* to go. Cliff called and asked about Talkeetna Air Taxi. He also phoned Cathy about Lowell Thomas' passengers. Mike Helms called from 17500 feet. He does not know what happened at 18000 feet. Eight left from 17500 feet about an hour ago to try to make contact with *Mountain Trip Traverse* and the Austrians, and will relay what is happening up there. The next contact is at 12:00. I called KES7604, got hold of Roger of NPS, and relayed information about the activity above. NPS advised that all Chinooks are grounded (no high altitude capability available). The highest capability is 14000 feet on the West Buttress, 15000 feet on the Harper Glacier. *Wolfgang* (three) 17000 was with *Mountain Trip Traverse* last night, but did not see McCartney and Kandiko. *Wolfgang* made the summit. *Mountain Trip Traverse* should be between Denali Pass and the summit. Also, I advised Mike Helms that the Chinooks are grounded.

Kamuros (Kamuro, Ueegime) from Japan, flew in with Cliff Hudson to do the West Buttress; they have no radio. Ollie called about the weather for scenic flights. *Health Club* (four), Minneapolis, Minnesota, flew in with Doug to do the West Rib (Steve Friddle, Rick Nelson, Tracy Holland, Paul Dvirnak). Doug did a flyover for the NPS, and tried to contact Helms—successful. He found two people on Cassin at about 18900 feet, going down and waving ice axes. He also should see three climbers (*Tokyo Unryokai*) about 2000 feet below. He said it looks like something is moving down on the Cassin. Mike reported to Doug that they (McCartney and Kandiko) have no food. Both are waving ice axes and moving; he cannot spot the Japanese team. Doug contacted *Mountain Trip Traverse* on the Ruth Glacier; they need to be picked up. Doug, talking to Mike from the air, says they need about one and one-half hours. Now someone has a problem, but does not want a rescue. Roberts and Helms do not want to be flown out. Mike discusses with Doug about the Japanese helping out with McCartney and Kandiko. Mike will descend with Roberts and Wolfgang Meyers (different Wolfgang) of *Mountain Trip Traverse* who is at 14000 feet with very bad frostbite. He requested that Doug ask *Mountain Trip Traverse* if they want to go down with Helms. Mike wants to know if there is a doctor at 13000 feet. He is advised to talk to Brian. Doug asks if *Mountain Trip Traverse* is going down the Harper. Lowell Thomas, in the air, asked the location of Brian of the *Genet* party, *Ireland* (two: Billy Ireland, Ulf Bjornberg), and John Svenson of *Mountain Trip Traverse*.

Glacier Slugs went up to 14000 feet, then back to 10500 feet overnight. *Infinite Odyssey* is at 13000 feet. I asked Brian to contact NPS. *Radke-Coghill* (six) USA, flew in with Hudson to do the West Buttress. They'll use Channels 14, 11, 19. They are Martin Radke, Ryle Radke, Tom Coghill, Dick Leonard, Steve Miller, and Jim Mahoney. Tom Coghill was in my calculus class. Nancy to Verne: "Congratulations, we are going to be at 14000 feet tomorrow night." I did a radio check with *Radke-Coghill*. *Twin-Cities* is at 12000 feet and moving up. Mike Helms is at 17000 feet and called about Wolfgang Meyers at 14000 feet; he talked to Nick Parker. Doug is going to fly to 14000 feet tomorrow to pick up Wolfgang Meyers, who has the frostbite.

Someone tried to call; sounded like the Austrians, the Swiss, or the Germans. The skip is very high. *Kenya 80* (two) is back for Hudson. *McGill*, at 17000 feet, called *Genet* at 14000 feet, to tell Cliff that the Italians are at 14000 feet. I relayed a message to Brian to call NPS at 16200 feet. The *Colorado Cuties* (three) are back. Cliff will not be in tonight because they are working on his airplane. The brake was not good on landing in Talkeetna; the plane went into a rut and flipped around. Tom down-powered, but the last flick of the prop hit a car. They replaced the prop; there was no damage to the car and no one was hurt. I asked KES7604 if the *Colorado Cuties* contacted either Hudson or Doug. Cliff and Sunny will work out whether *Mountain Trip Traverse* will fly with Hudson or Doug. Tokositna relayed to Boyd at Montana Creek through KES7604. Roy said an airplane would be in at 1:00 or 2:00 p.m. to pick up. Sunny was in and out; brought *Fineout* (three) USA, *Talkeetna* (two), *Michigan* (one) to do the West Buttress. They'll use Channels 9, 14, 19, (Doug) with Roy Davies' equipment. Dave Strubler, Larry Buskirt, Jane Griffith.

June 23. Cliff called. I need white gas. Cliff will be in at 11:00 a.m. *McGill* called from 17200 feet. He thinks Roberts and Helms are at 14000 feet. He does not know the location of McCartney and Kandiko, but will try to find out what the extra tent is at 14000 feet. Cliff called; Doug is not flying today. The Super Cub is better for 14000 feet, but they should get Wolfgang down to 10000 feet. The cost at 14000 feet is $1800 (for high risk flying at Windy Corner or lower). The cost is approximately $800 (base rate); cost for 10000 feet is about $1000.

Mountain Trip Traverse (six) is at Denali Pass and made their last radio contact. Nick Parker and Wolfgang Meyers will get to 14000 feet today and then to Base Camp. Please advise if *RMI Traverse* came back to Base Camp. *Mountain Trip Traverse* made the summit. They asked about the Czech tent as they thought it was out. If not they will move to 15000 feet. I relayed a message to Nancy with *Glacier Slugs:* "I miss her and good luck on the summit." Sunny (74F) called from the air, came in and out, is going to the Ruth Glacier. Mike Covington is going to come in. I told Sunny (via relay from Boyd at Montana Creek) to make a trip if possible and get the boys out (the mechanics). Don't bother with the parts, bring them out later. We need from Talkeetna: tobacco, papers, mail for Billy Ireland. I asked about the Hazen skis (if they belonged to *Swissmiss*). Bonnie will tell Sunny. Doug is to go to Talkeetna and Cliff has gone to Anchorage to get parts because the brake system is not right on one wheel. The Tokositna job is done and the weather is starting to lift there.

The German traverse group called from the top, and *Donauworth* read them loud and clear. Scott called, Sunny will be in in about 45 minutes. Jack Roberts is walking out. McCartney and Kandiko are still descending. They got the Czech tent off the Harper Glacier. Wolfgang is to be flown out from 10000 feet. Dan from NPS to come in soon. *Fineout* is at 7700 feet. *Wickwire*, USA (Jim Wickwire, Stimson Bullitt, both Seattle), flew in with Doug to do the West Buttress. Brian is at 17000 feet and needs a helicopter at 14300 feet for Wolfgang, McCartney and Kandiko on the Cassin. Roberts, Helms, Nick Parker, and Wolfgang are at 14300 feet. Two *Colorado Cuties* are going to 14000 feet. At 17000 feet are *Aspen-Denali* (five), *Mountain Trip Traverse, Donauworth* (three), and the Italians. Sunny will start by 10:00. I relayed about the helicopter pickup needed at 14000 feet. Brian is at 17000 feet. At 14000 feet, Wolfgang's frostbite has broken open. Ollie called and requested they coordinate with Brian and bring Wolfgang to lower altitude if possible.

June 24. *Cascade* is on the West Rib at 16480 feet. The cloud level is about 17000 feet, clear to 10000. *Cascade* said the ceiling is lowering to 16500 feet, but they can see that the plateau and Windy Corner below are open; the general cloud level is 13000 feet to the west, and across Windy Corner toward Kahiltna Pass, there are no clouds. Kahiltna Glacier is socked in. *Cascade* is looking at the plateau and the cloud level is at 17000 feet, Windy Corner is open, but is proximately limited. To the north of Windy Corner there is a break opening and closing all the way to sea level. Tents and the plateau are visible at 13500 feet. Kahiltna Pass is open. *Wolfgang* (the Austrian party of three, not Wolfgang Meyers) came back. *Cascade* is now fogged in with visibility 200 feet and the plateau barely visible. They can't see Windy Corner or Kahiltna Pass. Fog comes and goes. We synchronized our watches.

Talkeetna called for a radio check on CB. Talkeetna is coming through loud and clear. I broadcast to establish a radio relay through 16500 feet on the West Rib—talked to *Cascade* about their schedule to be picked up. They want contact every four hours. *Lady Sunflower* called about the weather for Talkeetna Air Taxi. There has been a slight improvement down there. Brian, at 17000 feet, advised that Wolfgang is stable. *Donauworth* (three) and *Austrian-Denali* are at 17000 feet, descending. *Bottoms-Up* (three) and *McGill* are at 17000 feet, ascending; *Colorado Cuties* (two) are at 14000 feet. Had a radio contact with Stan Brenner (at 14000 feet) of the *Genet* party; he is the son of the man who had the stroke or heart attack earlier. NPS, Dave, wants to talk more to Brian about the bodies. Messages relayed between 16000 feet and 14000 feet: (1) Wolfgang is stable but cannot move; (2) weather is to be bad for two days; (3) number of people there is 22, they have enough food and fuel; (4) Stan Brenner of *Genet* will wait at 14000 feet; (5) next radio check will be at 8:00 a.m.

June 25. Gunnar came back with the *Anchorage Community College* group. At 14000 feet-16000 feet, winds are about 25 miles per hour. Nobody's moving at 10000 feet, socked in. I heard an Eskimo on the coast on the CB as though he was outside my tent. *Radke-Coghill* group (six) is at 8000 feet in a whiteout; they are going to make a carry. At 1:05 I asked if the Spanish team was coming in, and also about Gunnar. At 1:10, I talked to Verne at 17000 feet; he says that Wolfgang got his frostbite on the summit on June 22 in the morning, and that all ten toes are affected. Nick is not a doctor, but he thinks that Wolfgang has thrombosis or phlebitis in his legs and that the condition is serious. Wolfgang is resting and stable but cannot climb down. At 1:15, the NPS weather report was poor, but weather may be lifting tonight. There is no doctor at 14000 feet; a helicopter is on standby and will come as soon as possible.

Update from Verne: the Austrian team (three), *Mountain Trip Traverse,* Gunnar, and Sarah and Erica of *Colorado Cuties* are at 17000 feet. *Aspen-Denali* will try for the summit, four Germans are going up, and the *Genet* party is going to try. *Bottoms-Up* are at 17000 feet. The Japanese (four) are at 16000 feet going to 17000 feet. The Italians are at 14000 feet and seemed OK. Also at 14000 feet are the rest of the *Colorado Cuties,* the *Glacier Slugs,* Nick with *Wolfgang,* Roberts and Helms, and Stan Brenner. *Infinite Odyssey* and *Donauworth* (three) are going from 12500 feet to 14000 feet. *Valley-Denali* moved up to 11000 feet. At 2:10, Cliff talked to 16500 feet; he is going to use a fixed-wing to see if a helicopter can get in. At 2:28, *Twin-Cities* reported they will move from 13200 feet up to 14700 feet on the West Rib. I advised them to keep their radio on if they hear a plane overhead, and also that *Cascade* is above them. At 7:50, Cliff called and said the weather is not good enough. At 8:00, 14000 feet reported that tomorrow they will be out of medicine. Wolfgang may have phlebitis. From 16000-14000 feet it is clear on the plateau; cloud levels are 12500 feet and 18500 feet; wind is steady. From 16500 feet they can see up the West Rib. Winds are about five miles per hour. I will stay on until 11:00 p.m.; if weather looks considerably better at 14000 feet, I will monitor on the hour.

June 26.   1:00 a.m., *Donauworth* (three) and one *Colorado Cutie* are back. 1:30 a.m., Roberts and Mike Helms are back. At 7:15 a.m., I talked to NPS about Wolfgang's probable thrombosis. They need his vitals. A different type of helicopter is needed for thrombosis than for just frostbite. Upper clouds are at 16500 feet; at 17000 feet there are patches of blue towards Talkeetna. Lower clouds are at 13000 feet and it's socked in below that, but the plateau is visible, though misty, and it is calm on the West Rib. I got information through to 16500 feet about Sarah's skis, only they are missing at 14000 feet. *Water Buffalo* (two) borrowed two pairs of skis from *Swissmiss* because of frostbite and their need to get down to 14000 feet. *Swissmiss* borrowed one pair of skis from *Donauworth,* so *Donauworth* borrowed Sarah's skis. Now Sarah has no skis at 14000 feet. 8:06: The weather seems local; they can see Windy Corner from the plateau. I asked for 14500 feet to advise if they can hear Base Camp. I can call. I also tried to get the party at 13500 feet, which is going up. From 16500 feet, they can see down to the tents; the area to the east is large enough for landing. 8:14: I called Cliff for the weather. There are no fronts moving in, though some cloudiness and showers are moving in. I advised him of the seriousness of Wolfgang's condition. 8:55: I tried to raise 14000 feet. The next contact will be with 16500 feet at 10:00 a.m., because of the limited battery supply. Information needed: (1) condition of patient; (2) information about his phlebitis, (or thrombosis); (3) condition of his toes; (4) weather; (5) time check. Broadcasts through 9:06. 9:51: Carlos called from 16500 feet. At 10:00 Carlos could see the square they had stamped out for the landing; local clearing at

16500 feet. Away from the Mountain it appears to be clearing at 14000 feet. Radio check at 12:00, unless weather looks good at 11:00. Roger is on the air: landing strip must be 2500 feet by 75 feet, and 100 feet uphill must be smooth for a fixed wing landing.

I talked to Roger, NPS, and advised him of the procedure we set up because of limited battery supply at 16500 feet. Also, I advised that they have tried to get 13500 feet on the air for a back up. I asked him to advise whether 14000 feet can hear Kahiltna Base. Then I could ask them to relay information to Roger to save batteries. At 14000 feet they need (1) a fixed-wing landing strip; (2) condition of patient; (3) more information on phlebitis, and condition of patient's toes; (4) weather; (5) time check. At 11:00, 11:30, 11:45, and 11:50 I tried to call 14000 feet. At 11:49, 16500 feet reported that fifteen people are heading up the West Buttress from 14000 feet, the plateau just opened up, there is a cloud at 14500 feet. Another check at 1:30, and I talked to NPS on HF. Carlos, at 16500 feet, talked to Doug and NPS. 12:22 p.m.: 16500 feet called to say there are nine in the group heading down hill at 14000 feet.

1:10: Tom came in, but aborted on take off due to the sticky snow. Roberts, with the frostbite, stayed in the plane and they unloaded the two others to bring the plane uphill with a light load. Then they could take two passengers and luggage out OK. 1:30: Those at 16500 feet could see the group going down; seven-teem are going up (*Mountain Trip Traverse* or Italians). We arranged for a radio check at 4:00 if anything significant is happening, otherwise there will be a 6:00 check. Dave (NPS) and Steve Porter will be in soon with Doug. Dave (NPS) and Steve Porter came in. *Noname* (thirteen), a USA team from Colorado, came in with Cliff Hudson. They are going to do the West Buttress. The group includes John Gerber, Steve Poulsen, Dave Glaser. 2:05: Larry Graveling and Randy Dogenhower, mechanics at Tokositna called; they can see Huntington.

2:15: Kandiko called to say he is on the way down to 14200 feet with the Japanese. They are desperate for food and request an air drop. He has gone seven days without food. The Japanese are heading down the Japanese Couloir and they have little food left. The cloud level is at 10000 feet, clear above, calm. Kandiko borrowed the Japanese radio to make the call. McCartney is alive and well. He asked that we make a call to inform Kandiko's folks of the situation. McCartney is very weak, but stable, and able to walk. Ollie called and advised that Tom took off. I called Ollie about the food drop for Kandiko and McCartney. Nick Parker might also need food. 3:05: The NPS will drop food, fuel and medicine at 14100 feet on the West Buttress. A helicopter is coming from McGrath: Roberts wants the helicopter to drop food and fuel to McCartney and Kandiko. Mechanics on the Tokositna have one day of food left, and want KES7604 to relay that to Boyd and Talkeetna Air Taxi. 4:00: A call from 16000 feet. Finally, 14000 feet called. There are fifteen inches of new snow ar 14000 feet. Manpower (about fifteen people) is available there to prepare a landing strip for a fixed-wing. 4:15: I overheard *Twin-Cities* response. 4:30: The chopper is on the ground at 14000 feet. 6:48: Cliff called about the number of people to go out. 8:15: Tom came in and went out. Tokositna is calling. 8:32: Brian, at 17000 feet, called.

9:00: Radio check. *RMI-Jansport* (11), USA, arrived with Hudson to do the West Buttress. The group included Lou Whittaker, Allen French, Gordon Matthews, Gib Mann, Tom Gordon, Mike Jensen, Craig Perpich, Terri (unknown), Jamie Lane, Bob Schamburg, Bob Shaw. YST-Alaska (three) arrived with Doug to do the West Buttress/West Rib; they have no radio. They are John Grant, Donald Morrison, Bob Thompson.

June 27. Cliff called about the weather and air traffic. I relayed Louis' message for tent poles. June 27: 8:32 a.m.: Brian, at 17000 feet, says there are lenticular clouds outside the area at 16000 feet, high winds (30-40 miles per hour) out of the south above 17000 feet. They will try for the summit. 8:35: Tokositna (mechanics) called; the weather has been good from midnight until now. They are on their last day of food. 11:10: Cliff called to say Tom is seven miles out and coming in. NPS called to talk to Gerhard at Park Headquarters at 1:30. Somewhere in here the mechanics from the Tokositna got out. Now the climbers from the British Army Expedition are left there. Tokositna, Jim (from British Army Expedition), called and wants cigarettes and a weather report.

1:45: Cliff called. He talked to the British Army about an avalanche on Huntington; they are pretty shook up, but OK. They may try to get off the Mountain earlier than planned; will advise. NPS called with the weather: high pressure should last one or two days as reported from Savage River. Dave has a Park radio, which he'll leave here while he's on patrol. 2:05: Carlos, at 16400 feet, is looking down on clouds. Dave, NPS, wants to know about the Japanese climbers, and also wants to talk to Brian about the German bodies. 2:36: Tokositna called about the weather. They also said they were moving across the glacier. 4:26: *Twin-Cities* called for a radio check. 7:10: Cliff called about the Italians. Brian Sprunt of Seattle has mail; Andrea of *Kenya 80* group took Talkeetna Air Taxi out.

Thelma Smith (left), a good friend whose late husband worked with Frances in Boeing research, enjoys a day on the glacier.

Climbers obligingly hold up wing of disabled plane while repairs are made.

The man from Texas
needs to be flown out

May 15. I started out after my Japanese class; it was after midnight. Arrived at Park Headquarters at 4:00 a.m. and slept in the car until Dave woke me up at 7:20. I had breakfast there, then drove to Anchorage to pick up fuel and other items, and stopped to see Roy and Bonnie Davies and discuss radio problems. Then I drove to Talkeetna. I stayed at the NPS station and met Father Dumfy, who is well known and has spent a lot of time in the bush, and who also spent three months up at the Mountain House, which Don Sheldon built. Charlie Porter and some others saw Father Dumfy up there.

May 16. There are good records of the climbing groups on the Mountain. I talked to Scott, the ranger there, who is doing an excellent job. I waited for Cliff to come back. The weather is closing in. There are Japanese and Korean parties on the Mountain. A Chinese party is going to come in.

May 17. I took off for the Mountain. We came in toward the southeast ridge of Foraker where Gary Bocarde is, but the ridge was socked-in. I arrived at Base Camp around 2:30 p.m. I had to reset the tent as they didn't know how to set up a single-walled canvas tent with seven-foot birch poles. Five of us got in together and moved the radio gear and the generator. Finally, I settled down somewhat. No more flights. Weather has been good on McKinley, but Foraker has had problems.

May 18. It snowed slightly, temperature is around 32 degrees Fahrenheit, there is no wind, the ceiling is at 7500 feet, and visibility is one-half mile. The radio is performing badly. HF doesn't work and CB reception is different (different antenna, and I think, as Roy suggested, that the main problem with the CB radio is the antenna). I talked to Gary at 13000 feet. Talked to John Svenson at 17000 feet on McKinley on the descent. He expects to be at Base Camp day after tomorrow. We arranged a schedule to talk at 7:30 p.m., and for a three-way communication with Gary. I asked John to keep his eyes open for possible problems on the descent. At 4:00 p.m. John called: 15000-foot cloud level, north side clear. I talked to Talkeetna. Doug will try to come in. Doug came in and went out; he barely made it as the fog rolled in. 7:30 p.m.: I talked to Gary, one tent is taking a beating. No change up there. John is also on the air. It's nice to talk to all these guys I know.

May 19. Gary was on the air at 7:28 a.m. Winds are 30-50 miles per hour. They plan to dig a snow cave because of the bad tent. Muggs is at Base Camp and helped with the generator. Gary called; they are all in the snow cave, and may need to send out messages tomorrow if the storm continues. At 8:01, I tried to call Mike Covington on the West Rib. Gunnar Naslund is in his party. Mike was on the West Rib last year when I came in. I've known Gunnar for several years. He is a good leader and he was in Valdez when we were on tour and he came to our concert. The weather report earlier indicated a front extending from Kotzebue to Cordova. Winds are from the south at 15000 feet.

May 20. Gary called. If there is no change in the weather by Thursday evening, they will have to descend on Friday. Gary wants to talk to John Svenson. Gary has enough food, but they're low on fuel.

May 21. 8:00 a.m.: I talked to Cliff; there's not much improvement in sight for the weather, but the sun is shining in Talkeetna and light cumulus are building up. 10:02 a.m.: Gary called; the winds have subsided and the clouds are moving in and out. They will start back tonight for the base of Foraker. Muggs fixed the generator today. 2:05 p.m.: Jay called. The weather is marginal but he will try to get in. There are crowds of climbers in Talkeetna trying to get in to McKinley. Jay came in and took Susan out. Other parties are leaving or coming in. Roger (NPS) is moving up to 16000 feet. I relayed that the Kennedy party needs two CBs in four days. Mike Kennedy and Chris Landry are going to ski the West Rib. The Koreans are at 16000 feet. Doug is in the air and going up to see and talk to a party with frostbite. Ed, who works for Cliff, broke the landing gear while trying to turn in deep snow. There were no passengers in the plane. I radioed out for Ed's pack to be sent in. Then I cooked something for Ed, and saw that he had a tent and sleeping bag. John Svenson called about the train schedule. Lowell Thomas relayed that the frostbite victim is walking to Base Camp. Part of the *Index* party returned. I talked to Roger at 16000 feet on the West Buttress. The *Genet* group is at 17000 feet. Mike Covington called; they are going to summit day after tomorrow. *RMI* (Horiskey) came back to Base Camp.

May 22. Bright clear day. John Svenson is returning with an art critic from Chicago. Cliff called. Boyd is coming in soon to repair the landing gear. I fed Ed some breakfast. Roy Davies is going to come in to work on the radio equipment. Lowell Thomas, Jr. came in with Cathy (*Genet Expeditions)* and Roy Davies. Gary Bocarde got down to the base of Foraker at 3:00 a.m. He will leave around 12:00 noon for Base Camp. He said the descent was very spooky: five to six feet of loose snow. I advised Cliff that Base Camp needs two-by-fours for guys for the radio antenna. Radio equipment is now ninety percent better. Roy brought the antenna. Dave, from South Africa, climbed the antenna to replace the upper portion on the tower. It's nice to see Roy. Beautiful day.

Dahl (four) is back and waiting for Talkeetna Air Taxi. Cliff called to find out if Muggs could use the South African vehicle. Cheesmund said that the starter is broken so it can't be used. Boyd is here with Larry to fix the airplane. Larry was one of the mechanics stuck on the Tokositna last year. Ed and Boyd left when the airplane was fixed. Mark Frenert and Rich Page returned. Rich is to fly out. Rich, who was a leader for Covington last year, said there are two South Africans and some Koreans with Mike. Cliff said to fill up the hole where repairs were made to the plane. Lots of dirt and oil were left on the snow, which will cause a melt problem. Mike Covington went to 17000 feet.

May 23. Two climbers came in for Cliff. They are Jeff Word and Taylor Lunis, and they reported that a man in Jon Waterman's and Steve Gall's group (leaders for Covington) nearly collapsed at 8000 feet. The man, who is from Texas, needed to be flown out, along with his wife. Their son will stay. Cliff called and advised of a problem at 8000 feet. Scott, of NPS Talkeetna, was called and advised of the problem. Doug called. He has a ski problem and must return to Talkeetna. It will take one or two hours for repair. Rich Page and Mark Frenert had seen a man and a woman on their return to Base Camp last night about 6:30. They were moving very slowly. Also they had found a cache belonging to *Radford (*three), and had brought it back to Base Camp, as they thought *Radford* had lost their cache. Steve Gall is here with a note from Jon Waterman advising of the medical procedure he had followed, the description of the patient's behavior and an explanation of his decision.

I called Scott, NPS Talkeetna, to relay information as a red plane flew past on the lower Kahiltna. It was probably Doug in Don Lee's plane, as Don has no radio and I could not make radio contact with the plane. I relayed contents of the note to Scott. Contents of note: About 6:30 p.m. yesterday the client collapsed with a breathing problem. Diagnosis: exhaustion. Administered fluids, rest and Valium. He is Ernest Chandler from Texas. He has pain in the left quadrant when he breathes deeply and he has a headache. He also has chronic high blood pressure. Pulse was 92 last night; this morning it was near normal, 68. Condition is stable—not a case of a dying man—but breathing was limited and painful last night. Decision: it would be a hazard for him to walk back four-and-a-half miles to the landing strip. Flight request is Jon Waterman's decision (client wants to try and walk it). Because his collapse was so severe, it can't be risked by walking him anywhere. He was carrying virtually no load, he could not manage a load at the time of collapse. Would like him flown to doctor, wife to accompany (refuses to stay). Site identity: single blue dome tent just before junction of Northeast Fork; stamped X in snow. Pulse and respiration are now normal and no coughing. Signed, Jon Waterman, Emergency Medical Wilderness Technician, Fantasy Ridge.

Cheap Canadian Climbers Club (two) Pat Paul and Dick Muter are back. I called Cliff; there are four of his to go and one for Talkeetna Air Taxi. Ollie relayed to Cliff in the air. K0714 (NPS) Talkeetna called regarding weather in Kahiltna Pass. Jim Wickwire is there and sends his regards and, also, he will send a letter with details of his climb (they were to do the Wickersham Wall). I advised that I had a letter here for Chris Kerrebrock. NPS said to send it to them. Don Lee came in and said that Chris Kerrebrock had died in a crevasse yesterday on the Peters Glacier. K0714 called in as they came through the pass in a helicopter on the way to the Peters Glacier.

Radford (three) came back and were mad because their cache had been picked up. They were ready to kill the party that picked it up. I told them that the party that picked it up thought they had lost it. Cliff called: there are ten with *RMI* to come in. Marty Hoey is the leader (very strong lady), and is to bring in the Bass family from Dallas, Texas (oil people). Jon Waterman is back with the wife of the evacuated man. Don came in and brought some of the *RMI* group. I finally got Jon Waterman aside and Don told him about Chris. Jon was a friend of Chris Kerrebrock's and the news was very hard for him, but we thought it better he learned it at Base Camp instead of by hearsay higher on the Mountain. Jon has had a bad time the last twenty-four hours, but he is OK.

Neil Glutchman of *Pics in Space* is back. Sean Meehan is on the way. Don brought in the last of Nick Parker's group, plus Muggs and two friends came along for the ride. Don is concerned about Mike Hill and Monte Westlund originally from *Boys on the Cassin and Hunter (BOTCH);* he's not sure whether they went to do the Cassin or not.

May 24.   I called NPS and talked to Dave about the records of the Japanese, an address for Jim Wickwire, and the whereabouts of Monty Westlund and Mike Hill of *BOTCH.* Brown, from 17000 feet, wants Talkeetna Air Taxi to reserve rooms for fifteen of *Genet* party when they come down. At 14000 feet, Alfred Agary relayed with group at 17000 feet. *Fantasy Ridge*, with Jon Waterman, is going from 9500 feet to 10000 feet. A lone climber at 14000 feet can't find his group. His name is Gosney, and he was to meet them two days ago on the West Buttress at 14000 feet. His party, James Garrett and Thor Kieser were on the Cassin. Mike Covington called; he was on the summit yesterday. They are starting down and will be at Base Camp tomorrow. The *Koreans* are on top today. *Genet* party (Alfred) is on the radio; Gosney has joined three Canadians (Horveth, Smith and Gillman) on the West Buttress to look for Garrett and Kieser.

Reservations for eleven have been made at the Swiss Inn in Talkeetna for the *Genet* party. I asked Cathy to make these reservations. *Uncalled For* (four) is at 14000 feet and looking good. Sean Meehan and Neil Glutchman saw Garrett's skis at 11000 feet quite awhile ago (nine or ten days). Don Lee came in with Lewis Leonard to catch Stuart McPherson and Ward, who left this morning for the West Ridge of Hunter. Roger called from 17000 feet on clean-up; he was on the summit yesterday with his party and will not do the traverse, but will be back in several days. He built a large rest room at 17000 feet, and wanded the way to a crevasse for garbage disposal. Roger called and advised of the following: Mutt and Jeff (Stacy and Curt) left May 13 for the Cassin, and have not shown up yet. They had only 13 days food. Also he needed a weather report.

May 25. *Denali Upper Mountain Bunch (DUMB)* called from 8800 feet. The Japanese group is going up. Four from Seattle came in for Hudson. They saw Monty Westlund and Mike Hill. I talked to Roy; he said sunspot activity is high, and usually comes in three-day cycles. Lowell Thomas was in and out; he picked up Monty Westlund and Mike Hill. Both the *Genet* party and Covington's group are OK at 10000 feet and are planning to return in the afternoon. I cannot raise the Koreans on Channel 11. The *Genet* group is arriving. I talked to Cathy; she wants Andy, Peter and Stephen to go first. I got Lady Sunflower to relay messages to Roberts to send mail to Sean Meehan and Neil Glutchman, and to Talkeetna Air Taxi to come for three Koreans.

May 26. Peter Carter of *Junior Set Club* is to go out. I asked Lady Sunflower to relay a message for Mark Frenert. Sometime later, Boyd (mechanic from Montana Creek) with his wife and her brother came to see the Glacier and eat lunch. They left a lawn chair. Roger called from 14000 feet and requested the number of climbers on the West Buttress. He also requested a flyby of the Cassin (two or three parties are missing). Doug came in with three visitors, and then attempted the flyby of the Cassin. Doug is at 17000 feet and can't see anyone coming down. Tracks are faded out above 17000 feet. Doug is coming down; he is having difficulty breathing and has a terrible headache. Lowell Thomas came in with two Australian cameramen, from one of the major companies, I think.

Roger is at 14000 feet; one German, Wolfgang, is coming down with them as he has frostbitten feet. Curt and Stacy are with them. Jim and Allen are going up the West Buttress at 14000 feet. James Garrett and Thor Kieser may be in trouble. Roger requested two or three flybys on the Cassin, and also a food drop. Roger will descend to 10000 feet or 11000 feet.

May 27. Cliff, Doug and Lowell Thomas all called about the weather. Forecast: scattered clouds in low valleys, several lows moving in, weather may deteriorate by the weekend. *Kimbel* is coming in; they are three Germans from Bavaria. Mike Kennedy's radio channel is 14A; Chris Landry's radio channel is 19B. The message on the Kennedy-Chris Landry cache is "Don't remove until 6-10-81". The cache is at 14000 feet (there is no fuel in it but there is fuel in the *Genet* cache).

There is a good set of tracks from 16500 feet on the West Rib to 14000 feet on the West Buttress. Their plan: to northwest fork tonight, then into northeast fork tomorrow with good forecast, then three days to the summit (Mike on Cassin, Chris on West Rib) then on the third day they'll come down the West Rib (Mike will climb, Chris will ski) to 16500 feet. They'll stay in an igloo, which is on the West Buttress side of the Rib against a rock, with food and fuel. On the fourth day they'll descend to 11000 feet on the West Rib, or, if conditions are right, go over to 14000 feet on the West Buttress and out the next day. Both have at least five days food, fuel and radio. Mike has a yellow Bibler tent; Chris has no tent. Chris and Mike left, took a picture with Mt. McKinley in the background.

NPS called about Garrett and Kieser. I advised him about Mike Kennedy going to the Cassin and Chris Landry to the West Rib. Dave Cheesmund is also on the Cassin. NPS requested I try to find out information about James Garrett and Thor Kieser, and Jim Mount and Dean Tinker: where they were last seen, what route, altitude, how much food on what date, any change in plans, how did they look when last seen, weather at the time last seen. I called NPS and advised Roger about two and one-half hours out. Also Dave said they made a recovery of a body on the Peters Glacier. *Gila Denali* is here, with one orange tent and one mustard yellow tent. *Havin No Fun* is to go out to the Ruth Glacier. Curt and Stacy last saw James Garrett and Thor Kieser at 15600 feet on the Cassin. Chris Landry relayed that Dave Cheesmund is going to return to Base Camp tonight; he was calling from the northeast fork.

May 28. Ollie called and I gave her a weather report from here: heavy dark clouds. Down there it is raining off and on, though it's better this evening. Korean party came in; one man is very sick. He became ill at 16000 feet: vomiting, high temperature, he needs to go to hospital. I suggested hot water and honey. He didn't appear to have the edemas, but seems more like flu. There is a lot of flu on the Mountain. His name is Lee Wong Yung (he was on the Everest expedition with the Korean who was killed here two years ago). I talked to Jack Anusewicz, who looked at him. It is not pulmonary edema. He listened and tested his abdomen, looked at pupils, which were OK. It is not cerebral edema. Probably a flu bug. Roger says there is a lot of flu on the Mountain. Jack Anusewicz said hot water and honey would be OK.

France (three) from the traverse are here for Talkeetna Air Taxi. *DUMB* is at 14300 feet. Everything is OK. Three returned from Hunter. Horveth is back with news that the two from the Cassin have been found. The Horveth party left them at 17000 feet. They are OK. Jon Waterman sends his regards.

May 29. K2 came in with three Austrians and went out with three from Colorado. K2 and Talkeetna Air Taxi came in and went out. They brought forms from Dave with a note. The University of Alaska, Anchorage, is doing research on high altitude-latitude climbers. They request that I try to get climbers' cooperation, and they will pay fifty cents a form. They sent 250 forms. The note also said they had recovered Chris' body, which took four rangers four hours, plus other details. *Van Tych* (two) came back and are waiting for Hudson; I got some wands from them. They are surveyors from Bellevue and Woodinville. We talked some; one knew Roscoe Carnahan and had worked for him a couple of years ago. I'm having trouble with the radio. I replaced one fuse in the CB. The HF is out of order. KES7604 says the Dallas family, Bass *(RMI)*, is at 14500 feet. Jay came in and flew out with *Van Tych*. I talked to Jay (in the air) about a scenic flight around the Mountain for seventy-five dollars for *Havin No Fun*.

May 30. I received your two letters the same day and thank you; the mail is getting slower and slower. In general the weather has been excellent, quite a contrast from last year. There are not quite as many climbers. A Korean group just went out. One of them came in very ill. I advised hot water and honey. After that he started getting much better. I have had several interesting talks with the Koreans. The South African lady has gone to Anchorage while her husband attempts to solo the Cassin. He left with a couple of black toes and injured thumbs. I really wonder if I'll ever see him again. I think his wife began to have some doubts about his climbing abilities after several of us were comparing goggles, and she found that her own glasses were very poor and that her husband had not used very good judgment in getting good ones for her. We played some games of Scrabble, which is fun, but the Koreans had a complicated game, which I would have liked to have learned.

The death of Jim Wickwire's friend, Chris Kerrebrock, was tragic. Jim wrote me a note, and it was a miracle that Jim, with a broken shoulder, ever survived. It was impossible for Jim to help Chris; he tried for five hours. It took four people from the

NPS four hours to recover the body. Jim and Chris fell about forty feet down into a hidden crevasse at 16700 feet on the Peters Glacier. Jim waited eight days on the Peters, and when Doug couldn't get in for a pickup, he started back toward Kahiltna Pass. Doug spotted him six days later. Jim was in a last ditch effort to get back over the pass, and down onto the Kahiltna. He had only a little dry food.

I don't know how much you have heard about Jim. He was, not now, one of the attorneys in the John Davis business. He now has his own firm. On K-2 he suffered lung damage, which resulted in a grim descent and finally in a major operation. Last year, here on McKinley, he was hoping to make the top to see if he could tolerate high altitude and test his endurance. He didn't look well, but later, according to everyone in Seattle, had made a remarkable recovery. Jim was slated to go on the next Everest trip and Chris was to have been deputy leader.

There are many French and Germans on the Mountain, plus four Japanese parties. I have heard that there is one Chinese party to come and a Mexican party has registered, but NPS feels they may not show up. I have been pretty busy up here and sunspot activity has been high this year, although things really do not seem that much different than the last four years. I keep meeting many of the guides and climbers that I have known over the years. John Svenson drew a cartoon for one of the climbing magazines and I'm in it. Apparently I'm known through most of the international climbing world—seems weird.

Karl and Anne may come in one of these days; I hope so. I'm afraid my clothes will be in rags by the time I get out. I brought four pairs of knicker-socks, two pairs have holes already. My knickers are beginning to look threadbare. Don brought in four little spruce trees yesterday and a little yellow warbler came along and sat in them for a short time. There were a few Gray-crowned Rosy Finches here. No one can figure how they get enough to eat. I have six weeks yet to go.

DUMB is at 14000 feet; so are *Mountain Gads,* two Japanese and one other group. Steve (with Covington) is going to 15000 feet today, and hopes to be up in four days and back to Kahiltna Base in six days. He will go to 17200 feet tomorrow. *RMI* is at 14000 feet, going to 16200 feet tomorrow, and to 17000 feet the next day. Four came in for Talkeetna Air Taxi: *Highland Fling* (two English, two USA). Chris Landry is on the West Rib at 16000 feet. Mike Kennedy is at 14000 feet on the Cassin.

I asked about the South African climber who was last seen entering the Japanese Couloir. *DUMB*, at about 16000 feet, is socked in. Jim and Alan are going to the summit tomorrow; they are now at 17000 feet. *Uncalled For* (four) is going to summit tomorrow; they are now at 17000 feet. Jon is at 14000 feet; I relayed that he has mail at Kahiltna Base. They asked that we keep Steve's ice saw here, as well as any mail for Nick Parker and Jon Waterman. *Talkeetna Locos* are coming in to 14000 feet—interrupted by Air Force rescue helicopter going over to the Brooks Glacier.

May 31. Mike is at 14000 feet on the Cassin. They will try to go up tomorrow. Chris Landry is at 16000 feet and will go to the summit day after tomorrow. Roy Davies says winds out of the northeast are going to be very high and may reach 80 knots; this information came from Fairbanks tonight on the weather forecasts. He also said that the low channel on the radio is better in bad conditions. Tonight Channel 14 is better than Channel 19. Roy also said to keep the batteries warm.

June 1. I talked to Lowell Thomas from KAB7929 (home). Talkeetna Air Taxi has thirteen to come in. Cliff called about the fuel and wands that Cathy wanted. She needed wands and thought some were for sale here; she also thought fuel here was for sale—negative. K-2 called about the party across the glacier on Foraker. They are a French group. Cliff called about Horiskey *(RMI)* and their cache. He also advised that Marty's *RMI* group has a ham contact at 6:00 p.m. and 4:00 a.m. He needs Lowell Thomas to swing by the Ruth Glacier to pick up passengers. *RMI* found the Horiskey tents and Lowell Thomas relayed the message to Jay that the Horiskey tents are at Kahiltna Base; they were found in Marty's *(RMI)* cache. Lowell Thomas advised about the weather: One Shot Pass is closed, but Two Shot Pass is open. K-2 message: does John Svenson have a harness? Yes, but they need a large shovel. I relayed the request to Talkeetna. Data is needed for the *Chalk-Redpath* party. I called Talkeetna Air Taxi, as they left before signing through Kahiltna Base. *Fantasy Ridge* is at 17000 feet today. *RMI* is at 14400 feet and will move to 15000 feet tomorrow. No descents today.

June 2. Mike Kennedy is at 17000 feet and will be on the summit at 4:00 p.m. Chris will eat breakfast and then go ahead if Mike climbs. Wind is high on the summit. If they both go to the summit, they will then come back to the igloo at 16500

Frances and Claude Glenn prepare to begin hike.

The author, carrying heavy pack, ascends steep snow slope during successful 1964 ascent of Mt. McKinley.

81

Frances and Al Randall, on 1964 McKinley ascent.

Frances (left), with
Al Randall (below) on
McKinley's summit.

Climbing party on the Kahiltna Glacier.

Author with Mt. Frances in the background, named in her honor following her death in 1984.

Army high altitude exercises on the glacier.

85

Base Camp.

Television camera crew. CBS paid a visit.

87

Arctic Chamber Orchestra with director, Prof. Gordon Wright.

feet on the West Rib. Doug (Talkeetna Air Taxi) has a party to go to the Ruth Glacier, but he needs a flight to go in before he can take these people over to the Ruth. K0714 (NPS Talkeetna) is on the air: there is an emergency at 14000 feet. The German from Munich has pulmonary edema and needs a helicopter evacuation. They are in contact via VHF with a Talkeetna ham. I have good contact at 15000 feet and on up to 17000 feet. The Swiss guide (Michael Boos) has Dextron, which he will take with him on his way up, in case the helicopter can't make it in.

Ajex-Austrian (four) came back with one member who has pulmonary edema. I talked to *Ajex* here in Kahiltna Base. Lois Humenberger, an Austrian guide who has been to 21000 or 22000 feet in the Himalayas with no problem, is the one with pulmonary edema. Cliff called about the weather: local fog. K0714 called about the weather. They will be coming in with a chopper. Weather is fogged in at Kahiltna Base, but looks OK up high. K-2 is to fly over. I talked to Cliff about the order for *Mountain Trip*. Cliff is going to come in soon. Both Kitty and Kimbel of K-2 are here—also, photographers to photograph the descent of the West Rib on skis by Chris Landry.

Fantasy Ridge, two Scots, three French, and three of *Uncalled For* are to go to the summit tomorrow if conditions permit. K-2 was here and went out, with two Swiss, to the Ruth Glacier. They could not get in and up to photograph Kennedy and Chris.

Doug called about his girl friend, Karen, and her brother. They will have no tent tomorrow as Karen and her brother made only a carry with Brian and decided not to go on. The Bass group, with Marty *(RMI)*, came back together. The only radio in the area was the Bass ham radio. No other CB. Doug called about his girl friend and the weather. I advised that they need a pot and a tent. Also, the K-2 party of photographers (Art Twomey and Jim, editor of *Backpacker Magazine*) needs pots. I will lend them one of my two. Mike called from 19000 feet and is waiting. D. Cheesmund of South Africa is there, also. They will start for the summit today at 4:00 p.m. The German evacuated yesterday has been stabilized, but was not in good condition upon arrival at Providence Hospital in Anchorage. *Uncalled For* (four) will try for the summit today. *Fantasy Ridge*, the French and the Japanese are also at 17000 feet.

June 3. I talked to Cliff. Jay has cooking pots in the airplane. *DUMB*, at 17200 feet, called about the weather; they are in a whiteout, light snow. Three Japanese are there, and a large party of Japanese are going up. *Fantasy Ridge* is going up; three French are climbing (one came back with cold feet); Jim is climbing; three from Anchorage are climbing. Gary's group lost one pair of orange crampons. Gary and John left. *Fukuoka* (eight) came in for Hudson. The German, who was evacuated yesterday, was in intensive care, but is doing fine. He is to be released tomorrow. Gosney, Kieser, and Garrett should arrive back at Base today. Gary Bocarde is at 8000; no one else is there. He gave me a weather report for up to 17000 feet and came in loud and clear from his location. Nick Parker is at 14000 feet; everything is OK and they will move to 16000 feet tomorrow. Chris Landry wants to meet Mike Kennedy on the West Buttress at 14000 feet. Mike, is on the West Buttress at 17000 feet. Chris skied down the West Rib to 16000 feet, but will not go down the rest of the route because the conditions are terrible. David is with Mike.

Doug called about the weather and his girl friend. I fed her and her brother here. Doug tried to get in, but had to turn back. His girl friend and her brother are in the red tent. The Austrians are under their tarp. They dug a snow cave.

Things here are terribly hectic. At the same time that the German was being evacuated yesterday from 14000 feet, an Austrian, who was a guide and had been to 21000 or 22000 feet in the Himalayas, was brought to Kahiltna Base with pulmonary edema. He was not bad off, but the German almost didn't make it. Some Australian television people were back again, and I'm in the Lowell Thomas thing for Alaska, which will be in Australia. The other day, Lowell Thomas brought in some friends from the East Coast who are friends of Brad Washburn.

The guides for *Mountain Trip*, Gary Bocarde and John Svenson, came back to lead another climb. Gary was on the American team in China this last year, and John is a cartoonist. They had a very interesting team this time: a doctor, a physicist, and also, the owner of the California Press, who said he had heard a lot about me. Interesting! Anyhow, now the editor of *Backpacker* and a photographer are here. The latter man has been all over the world and has done some fascinating climbs and explorations. He suggested that I try to get a job in the Antarctic with one of the research groups. It would mean being gone for six months, which I don't want to do, but it also would mean I could see South America. I doubt if I'll do it, but it would be a change. I was practicing this morning and then he took a bunch of pictures of me playing on the Kahiltna with all the different mountains in the background, so I think (hope) I'll get a nice photo.

June 4. For mountaineering news: Chris Landry did ski the West Rib. I have been the radio link for Chris and Mike since they were on opposite sides of the Mountain. Two pairs of my knicker socks have got holes in them and I had only one pair left, so, finally, one pair was located in Talkeetna. Oh yes, one of the Koreans got the flu (he had been on an Everest team) and was terribly ill from upset stomach, dehydration, etc. So I advised hot water with honey and he started to improve. I had some interesting talks with them (and I hope I didn't write this before). In the radio log, I keep track of dates, but I have not been doing so in this letter.

June 5. I tried to get a lesson with Kathy before I left, but she didn't show up. Also, she wanted me to work on the Mendelssohn because she was going to play it, and I really do not want to because of this. I'd much rather do Lalo. John Svenson wired my cassette tape recorder to the battery so I can listen to music without burning up little batteries. There is a flute in one of the parties on the Mountain and I hope we can play a duet, as I brought along some Bach duets for two violins, which we could play. Another climber, who played the road bands, left his trumpet with me. He was very hurt because a ham radio operator, in the next camp to his here, complained that the trumpet was disturbing his radio waves.

There are some very extreme climbers and skiers here. A French team skied down the southeast ridge of Foraker and will do the same on Crosson, which is not as much of a feat. The Kahiltna is surely different from any place else, and I'm busier than ever. Dale is forwarding my mail, which takes over a week to get here. Netcko writes that Foxy is happy playing with her dog, and I got a letter from Iola and one from Aunt Mary.

June 8. I certainly have little time to write, it seems. The last plane came in at midnight. The weather this year has been much better than last, and I think the number of climbers has increased remarkably. I have little time for reading or practicing. But, of course, I have met many interesting climbers, and I keep running into climbers that I have met before, plus I know most of the guides. Mike Covington is back again and he sent me some fresh vegetables from Wasilla or Anchorage, as did John Svenson earlier. Cliff brought in some frozen strawberries with cream the other night. I shared them with one of Mike's guides, who had to stay on the glacier and get things together before Mike and his party arrived. The South African lady and her husband have gone. I have interesting talks with the Koreans and Japanese. I still do not know if the Chinese or Mexican teams will arrive. The Germans seem to be having the most trouble with pulmonary edema, as they insist on climbing too fast for their acclimatization, and they refuse to listen to any advice from anyone about acclimatization. With the high latitude here, it makes McKinley equivalent to 23000 or 24000 feet. In the Alps, they are very used to climbing fast.

Chris Ruelry, from the Olympic Ski Team, and two companions tried to make the top and back within twenty-four hours. They ascended to 10000 feet and then came back in less than twenty-four hours, which is still excellent. In Mexico we climbed almost 6000 feet and back in about twelve to eighteen hours. Mike Kennedy and Chris Landry gave me a weather radio when they got back from their skiing and climbing trip. Lowell Thomas brings me the newspapers. The High Altitude is one of the organized groups we have here now. I have had very interesting discussions with a lady who is with them. I now have less than five weeks here.

June 10. Whenever it is quiet, things happen. Nick Parker has a sick person at 17000 feet, and will bring him down to lower elevation tomorrow. I just got a call from the *Northeast Fork*: one person in Cliff Beaver's party has had frostbite, bleeding between purple toes, blisters, and probably can't get his boots back on. With the help of the NPS team from here, which is going to the Northeast Fork, they can get him back to the bottom of the hill. Then recruits from here will help. Radio contact was established with NPS at midnight, and then later for a relay team. Also, I got another call from the Northeast Fork, but it was very difficult to hear with the high skip. It is probably the same problem, but I do not know. It should be covered by NPS and my contact with them. I met the editor of *Backpacker* and his photographer friend and climber, who has been all over the world. These two guys were pretty special. Art lives about two hours north of Avery in Kimberly, B.C., so I may see him in the next year or two.

So many things happen here, and I meet so many climbers,

I scarcely have time to write. I do not have the foggiest idea when Fathers' Day is. Lowell Thomas has not been by lately with the newspapers. When I left, the Fathers' Day cards were not on sale, so I bought birthday cards, but have not sent them yet. I'm trying to read more Guatemalan legends. Many French climbers have come through, and I understand quite a lot, but I need more verbs. My Japanese has come in handy, but I have almost no time to study. I was up before 7:00 a.m., and will be up most of the night, and then again tomorrow. This goes on and on and sometimes I'm pretty tired. Climbers and the pilots give me lots of food, so I'm never lacking.

I hope the pilots come across with more pay. A music teacher from Delta, who plays flute, was here and brought a recorder; and I had some Bach duets, so we played duets on the Kahiltna. The Bass family from Dallas climbed with Marty Hoey (lady guide) from *RMI*. The Basses know Byron Kidd, the oil man who was the step-father of Pat Chamay, who was on McKinley with us. (As you know, Pat later died on Rainier of pulmonary edema: a tragic loss).

June 16.   I received your letter and the flower. Thank you. At times, things are excessively busy here, and once in awhile I have a few moments of relaxation, but mostly the hours have been very long. Things are going along much better on the Mountain. There are many Japanese. A group from Osaka gave me green tea (very expensive) and some beautiful little cakes. The French team of eleven gave me a huge thermos, and people are also sending up fresh things, and the pilots bring me almost anything. Lowell Thomas usually brings the newspaper. I have lots of interesting talks with the guides and many climbers new and old. My picture is taken many times and a large portion of the climbing community of the world seems to know me or has heard of me.

The director of the University of California Press at Berkeley was through here. He said he'd be in touch, whatever that meant. And the editor of *Backpacker* was here, as I mentioned, and asked about an article, which we discussed. I suppose I ought to get with it and make some money. I hope to get to fly over the Peters Glacier, as I'd like to do a story about that tragedy. I had hoped that, for my senior project, I might write a series of stories about the Mountain in Spanish. I hope all is well and the garden is growing. Eleven Chinese are coming in.

June 17. Life on the Kahiltna goes on. Today, Lowell Thomas brought in a reporter who interviewed me. I think I spend too much time being interviewed and photographed. Anyway, later on, Gary Bocarde and John Svenson called from the summit and requested that I play the violin for them over the CB. I think that is a first for a summit party, being serenaded, and with the "Canzonetta" (the first part), as it was pretty cold up there. The weather has been very good, and about sixty-three percent of the climbers are getting to the top. It's incredibly beautiful here, and today we saw one of the largest avalanches ever come from near the top of Hunter. I'm sitting and listening to Paul play the Beethoven from several years ago. My tape deck is wired into the big battery, which is surely more satisfactory than using the small batteries that wear out very fast. I also have most of our last concert on tape. The Chinese are from Hong Kong and are very well organized and very nice. I talk to many Japanese parties on the Mountain. I just learned from Cliff that the Mexicans are coming in the afternoon tomorrow. I have met a very nice man from Idaho, whom we call H, and his buddy from Oregon. One of the guides from *Infinite Odyssey,* whom I have known for years, is here, along with a couple of Scots and various other people. I surely hope I get some climbing in when I come down—plus working.

June 21. Lowell just dropped some cookies and bread, which were sent over from Camp Denali. He is taking up sightseers from there and frequently drops in when conditions are OK. Today there is fog on the lower Kahiltna, but it blew out soon. Cliff has fourteen to come in, five of which are from Mexico. Most of the time I'm very busy, and am not getting all the things done I have wanted to do. I still have three weeks to go and have been here for five. So far, in five weeks, I have never been alone on this glacier. By the time I get out, my clothes will truly be in rags. I certainly will be glad to see Foxie and Sgook, and hope they are OK. People bring or send up fruit and vegetables, supplementing everything the pilots bring. So I hardly am wanting for anything.

Lowell Thomas brought a newspaper yesterday with all the news about the Alaska Legislature. The officials and big interests are grabbing all the money and wasting it; the people in the state are as poor as usual. They are building new roads, which most people can't afford to drive, and so far, are doing little to maintain the old ones. I finally received your letter. I have a small portion of the music lesson I recorded when I was home, Mother. So you are listened to along with the greats. Well, this is Father's Day, and I hope you got the cards in time. Since Father's Day usually occurs while I'm up here, I usually am unable to get cards, so I hope the revised birthday cards are OK. I must get some lunch and do some more work.

June 30.   I was just starting to write in the diary when two Chinooks arrived with the Army to climb the Mountain. I grabbed my camera to get some pictures, as it's quite a sight watching the Army arrive: getting out of the rear of the Chinooks, roped-up and stabbing for crevasses like the enemy was lurking in the snow. The Chinooks create quite a wind. Many things have happened, day after day. Mike Covington was finally sighted by Doug this morning; he was to have arrived around 5:00 a.m. yesterday. He lost three of four tents and two sleeping bags under twelve feet of snow. One man has a badly frostbitten foot. They should arrive by tomorrow afternoon. Then, one Japanese team on the West Rib had some problems: bad headache up high. They came down the West Rib to meet up with *WHAT* at 16500 feet. *WHAT* did not have the resources to take care of them, as they all had hypothermia, and one had possible symptoms of cerebral edema.

In the meantime, we have had terrible storms, high winds, heavy snowfall, cold weather and then warm temperatures: no stability anywhere. Finally, the weather cleared up, high enough and long enough for the Japanese to descend to 14000 feet on the West Buttress, with one member of the *WHAT* group, who had stomach flu. A three-way contact was maintained between Hongkong, *WHAT* and Kahiltna Base. *Osaka YMCA* (*OYMCA*), at 14000 feet on the West Buttress, and *Nibon Daigaka* (Japan University), could not join in the coordination, as they were Channel 2 and the others were on Channel 19. I have 1-40 channels. There is one doctor on the Mountain who is in that area, but I'm really worried about his medical advice from a previous epic on the Mountain, which I'll soon write about.

The *Mexican Gatos* are further down the Mountain and have a doctor who is excellent. I know four of their five from Mexico. Also, Patti is along, and hopes to be the first Mexican woman to climb to the top of McKinley. The Mexicans are quite a team and we have had a good time seeing each other up here and talking on the radio. The Mexicans had no sooner left Kahiltna Base, when I received a call from the NPS at 17000 feet. A member of the *Cascade Alpine School* had decided to take some very potent medication on his own after coming back from the summit. He had a touch of cerebral edema also. To get this one person down the Mountain required several delays in climbing schedules of probably fifty other people, the assistance of eight in Kahiltna Base to help drag him, thirty-six hours of radio work on my part, the attention of the pilots and the National Park Service, plus countless exhausting hours of the other climbers.

Just before this, one team who had seen edema before recognized that one of their members had it and immediately came down before he was so bad. He came out OK. So life has not been uneventful here. These storms now are bad: reminiscent of last year, and the cold. I've met some very interesting people and climbers, and there was a big write-up in the Anchorage paper with pictures about me. It's snowing and Cliff has fifteen to come in, Lowell Thomas has sightseers to come in. The NPS can't get in to the Ruth Glacier. Everything is tied up with the weather. The Army asked me if I knew anything about the weather, since their reports are bad. I said mine weren't good either unless we could get jet plane reports.

July 1. After the last letter I wrote yesterday, the Army came over. Two guys that had been here last year came over. The whole group seems very enthusiastic. They have a doctor and civilian advisor. The big colonel and the head of all the Alaskan forces is supposed to come in next week. There are seventeen. Major Cavanaugh sent his regards from last year. He was at the Pump House one Sunday when we were playing. Two guys are on loan from the Marine Corps. John Keiser is their leader and has two silver bars. Soon afterwards, John Keiser and another man came over because they couldn't get their communications to work, and they needed to get in touch with the military in Talkeetna.

I got hold of K-2, who has the only battery-operated radio in Talkeetna, which was useful yesterday when the electricity was off there. During this visit I had to get hold of the Japanese to ask them to call back at 9:00 p.m., and also the one remaining Scot returned the pie pan in which I had made cheesecake for Mike Covington's group. The cheesecake had to be eaten since Mike didn't arrive on schedule. Meanwhile, I received calls from Mike that he was an hour out, so I started heating water. They have been two nights with only one tent for ten people, and have lost two sleeping bags. K-2 called back regarding the Army Communications problem, which can't be solved until tomorrow. I got hold of the Japanese, who say they are coming in tomorrow and that the one American will be in tonight. *Gatos* were on the air but I couldn't copy; the skip is very high. Then Mike Covington came in dragging tremendous loads; one member has frostbite.

The Army, at least the new recruits, mostly stood amazed as Mike's group came in. The Army has two huge wall tents for storage and communications. Three of the seventeen are to remain behind. They have offered to put up Covington's group, and the doctor is going to help with the frostbite. They had to haul the frostbite victim on a sled most of the way. The Army took the frostbite victim up to their big tent and started thawing out his feet. The tent was so hot hardly any of Covington's group could stand it, nor me. Anyway, Mike's group is sleeping outside, and the member from *WHAT* is staying in the storage tent. It's still snowing and no one can fly. Now, there are thirty here. When the Japanese arrive, if the weather does not improve, there will be ten more here. They also have a frostbite victim today. I'll start melting a supply of water again. Guess this is all, as I have to start trying to get through to Talkeetna. The skip is still very high and I'm listening to some truckers somewhere. On the skip, I talked to Wainwright, Alaska (up by Barrow).

July 7. Yesterday, two choppers came in, for the Army, to pick up a radio and bring another in. Then, later on, the three Irishmen arrived. They left around one or two in the morning when the snow was hard. They are from the southern part of Ireland and we talked a lot. In exchange for some tent stakes, they are going to take me on a walk or hike in Ireland if I ever get there. One is from County Cork and another from County Laois. They wondered if I still had any relatives living there to look up, so I said I'd have to go back in the family tree. I listened to them talk some Gaelic and it was all really interesting, and somehow, I have to go to Ireland.

The Spaniards are here on the Mountain. They are from Valencia and I talk Spanish to them on the radio, while my ear is tuning into their special variety of Spanish, which is not pure Castilian. They are nice men, and we've had lots of talks about Spain. Of all the groups who come here, the Americans (some), the Scots and the Irish seem to be the poorest. I miss the Mexican climbers, but the Irish surely made up for it. I had a long talk with three Swiss before they flew out yesterday and one of them had a birthday. I have been extremely busy and have had little time to do all the things I have needed to do. Karl and Anne Eide are supposed to come up on July 10 and 11, just before I go out.

This season has been long and I have had more work as the number of climbers has increased, although now there are not so many on the Mountain. The weather is changing and it is getting colder. Until about two weeks ago, the weather has been remarkably good by comparison to last year. Since then, we have had some terrible storms, including in this area, with lots of new snow, producing extreme avalanche conditions. Soon I shall be able to see green again, although Don Lee did bring me some trees and Kitty sent a lovely bouquet of wild rose, ranunculus and blue bells.

Oh yes, a columnist was here from the *Boston Globe,* so I think I'm in there, too. I need to work, sew, practice and do some climbing when I'm done there. I'll probably spend Tuesday, July 21, in Seattle, so I'll get in late Monday.

NOTE: On July 19, a man from the Park Service called to say that planes hadn't been able to get to the glacier for nine days. Seventeen people were waiting to come out. Frances was all right, though. She called from the park the afternoon of July 22.

Nobuyoshi Chiba, who climbed McKinley and became a close friend, with wife atop mountain in Japan.

Chapter Seven — 1982

"Walter Cronkite was here with his wife"

May 30. 6:30 a.m.: Just a short note to let you know I'm OK. As you probably well know, there have been a lot of problems up here. There are more climbers than ever and the temperature has been about twenty degrees colder than average. The storms have been very bad and last a long time and the winds have been very high. The Mountain is mostly blue ice from 12000 feet to the summit. I'll try to write more later. Peter Habeler is here; we are friends. Also, I met a Basque from Basque. He speaks the language and also, climbed Everest with the Poles; we talked awhile. Then I spent a long time talking to an Ecuadorian who speaks several languages, plus his native Quicha. He has read a lot so I loaned him some of my Spanish books that I have here. He is a guide and there are only about two-hundred climbers in Ecuador.

June 10. I'm terribly busy and have attempted to write you diary letters, but it has been almost impossible. Thank you for yours and the news and the flowers. I hope Daddy quits falling down. Things have been terribly hectic here. There are more climbers than ever and the storms are worse than last year. I meet quite a few climbers that know Daddy and his train. Bob Plurie, from Wenatchee, and Haire, from Leavenworth, were here, and I still have one green mitten that they left behind, which I'll bring when I come down there. There are few people making the summit; it is totally impossible most of the time.

We have had some epic events this year. The worst was the two Japanese who fell from 18000 feet to 17000 feet to 16000 feet and were spotted by Brian Okonek just before another storm broke. They were rescued and taken to 14000 feet, to the Med Hut (medical research station) there. The older man had cranial bleeding from the nose and mouth. The younger had severe head injuries. They were put on IVs. The weather was terrible and Chinooks could not evacuate them. They ran out of IV fluid just as Peter Habeler came along with some more. That lasted through the storm and till about 5:00 a.m., when the clouds opened up and the Chinooks could come to the rescue. The clouds closed up several hours later and the storms have continued. The older man probably will not live, though he has maintained his own in a coma. The younger, whom I have known and have talked to in years past, is improving. He is a very good climber and leader, and I hope they both become well. I was on the radio for two days and nights. I have had little sleep most of the time.

Walter Cronkite was here with his wife for about one and one-half hours; hopefully, a picture of myself, Lowell and Walter will come out. CBS was over on the Ruth making a film. Lowell is trying to fly in now, but I don't think he can make it as the weather is bad. In any event this is all for now. I surely will be happy to see some sun and green grass and trees.

June 19.   I have been so busy that I haven't been able to do much on my diary to you, but I am working on parts of it. Briefly, on June 15, one of the guides for Mike Covington returned with a lady who had had a nervous breakdown. He had traveled several days almost non-stop to get her here, and to keep her moving, as she would wander off and want to jump off cliffs. He arrived here to find some forty-four people waiting in bad weather for the planes.

Life was quite an ordeal. She would quiet down, but injected Valium only worked for several hours at a time. We kept her in an area away from the rest of the people, and took shifts of two hours each, with two people per shift, to keep her from hurting herself or others. An Australian doctor, who was a real goon, really set her off to screaming and yelling, and I'm sure with good cause. So we had to convince the doctor to stay away from her. Then we ran out of injectable Valium and had to resort to oral Valium mixed in Tang. This ordeal lasted about thirty hours with innumerable psychotic episodes. This woman had a history of schizophrenia, breakdowns, etc., and was known to API in Anchorage. I was in continual communication with the pilots, and NPS; they, in turn, communicated with doctors and API. Her fiance had been killed in an avalanche several years ago, and she has never been the same since. Finally, Doug Geeting took his life in his hands and made an emergency trip in to take her out. The assistant guide, a nurse, and one other man accompanied her.

The pilot, Doug, brought in some more injectable Valium

to zap in-out in case she became violent in the airplane. She was convinced it was better to be in a sleeping bag in the airplane as she might get cold. This was preferable to the straightjacket, which was available. I had been in her presence when she came to after a couple of hours of "Hot Tang" and her eyes were rolling around. The first person she saw was the Australian doctor. She took a swing at him and knocked his glasses off. I hate to think what he would have done to her if I hadn't been there. Two of the other guys finally got her calmed down and we convinced the Australian doctor not to come near. Anyway, they got her to Talkeetna and into an ambulance to Anchorage. We were totally exhausted.

The next day, the weather cleared. Fifty-seven people flew out and thirty-four flew in. In amongst airplanes and people, a National TV crew flew in with Lowell. They televised the medical research unit and all the activity here. They also insisted that I play the violin so this should hit National TV sometime. It was hectic.

The next day, Jim broke some bolts in his landing gear, on the last trip he was to make, and we had to have Boyd, from Montana Creek fly in. About fifteen climbers acted as a human jack to hold the wing up while repairs were made. I have some pictures of this. Many people have been in avalanches. Mike Covington lost a lot of gear in one and arrived here last night, but everyone is fine.

I am having trouble with Jill, in my cabin. She kicked my cat and thought the apple box was kindling. They are antics. So I've asked the Park to contact the Chapins to take care of Sgook, and Dale to see if my cat and Foxie are OK. When I get off the Mountain, Jill is being kicked out of my cabin by me.

June 29. I have a little less than three weeks to go. I have been terribly busy and we have had the worst weather ever on this Mountain. The night before last, we had winds in this area gusting to 50 miles per hour and it shredded the tarp on my tent and blew out the front part of one side; so I had to throw snow on the sides to hold the tent down. The climber from Hong Kong, who had been to the top, had his tent break here in Kahiltna Base with the high winds. After several days of beautiful weather, it changed with extremely weird clouds as a harbinger of ill winds. One cloud formation near McKinley looked like the inside of a boomerang being pushed along through the sky. Layers of lenticular clouds came from the summit of the Mountain, and then Foraker, which seldom has lenticulars, developed them. The sky became filmy, dark and brooding, while Mike Covington was climbing on the direct West Buttress route at 15000 feet. He finally was caught in the wind, but did manage to tie his tents into some ice blocks on a forty-degree slope.

Muggs and I discussed communication problems. I've known Muggs for years also. He has a group of three top Italian guides and several others, which include one of Italy's top economists, who can't seem to cope very well with not being able to control the weather. Here the weather controls everything.

I'll try to get some more written. Things have slowed up a little. This year will show a record number of climbers on the Mountain and, so far, no fatalities; but we do not know the future. I have met a number of climbers who know Daddy and the train. I probably will be in another Alaska Magazine this next year sometime. I'm going to be exhausted by the time I leave. Thelma was here for about five days, and I was happy to see her, but also very busy. Do not send letters here after July 12.

June 30.　Today the weather cleared, and the Chinooks tried to put up the equipment, but could not as the down draft was too great. They did pick up equipment here for the medical research team, and I saw several of the crew that I had met before. Bill Strauss, the civilian advisor for the Army Mountain Troops who was here last year, was here again. He comes to some of our concerts and FLOT performances, all the way from Big-D, which is about one hundred miles away. The Chinooks sure look like "science-fiction-creatures" in the sky. Then several planes came in and the NPS crew of five flew out. I am always happy to see them as we have many notes to exchange on what is going on on the Mountain. This will be a record year.

The weather closed in after Cliff and Jim came in. Don was on his way in and nearly got caught in the ice fall with zero visibility; but he finally got out and Providence was on his side. The pilots are flying in even more marginal weather as the number of climbers has increased and the weather got poorer and poorer. Then the storms hit: high winds and snow. I now have a little over two weeks to go and it has been hard work this year. There are only a few here at Kahiltna Base, but more will come to fly out tomorrow and the weather will be bad. I have met the Basques again. I talked a lot with one group of two, and one young man gave me a flag, a book about Basque myths and a scarf from the Canary Islands. They invited me to come to Basque and see all the native festivals.

The Norwegians, who are very conservative and speak excellent English because they studied very hard before they came here, have invited me to go visit Norway. I told them that when I was very small, I used to go with my father to Leavenworth and watch their countrymen soaring through the air like gods with wings. The young man from Hong Kong made the summit and we discussed Eastern and Western differences in thinking processes. An Austrian couple was here. I played Mozart for them, and they invited me to Salzburg and gave me a nice brochure on the Mozartium there. One of the "Meds," a lady doctor from Fresno, had brought her recorder, so we played duets to a captive audience. It was strange to hear applause of mittened hands going "Klopt-Klopt." I think I'll be in a picture article in an Italian paper with the Italian group and the Italian economist.

July 1. The storm continued through the night with high winds and nearly a foot of snow. The wind wears on the rocks around the outside of our tents. A *Time Magazine* article about the misery of the rest of the world is alien, as the clouds and winds roar through the skies. Gary Bocarde's group of thirteen is back from Seminar. I talked to the two Mexicans from Mexico City. The young lady is strong and very quiet. I'm quite sure she will be the first lady from Mexico to climb McKinley, probably next year. I made arrangements with NPS and Dianne for a 4:00 a.m. weather check for the Chinooks to pick up gear at 14000 feet.

July 2. The weather is clearing, but it is much colder, so the brief summer is gone. I talked to NPS at 7:00 a.m. about the weather for the Chinooks to come in. Chinooks came in. Winds are starting to pick up. Cliff has eleven people to come in; Talkeetna Air Taxi has sixteen to go out. Don Lee is going to come in. I talked to the Chinooks on 3411. Everyone is working on an airstrip. Mike Covington will come down tomorrow. A friend of Boyd's, from Montana Creek, is in the air overhead. He has a cyclist from Hawaii with him and is showing him the country. Cathy is calling from 9000 feet. The rest of the *Genet* group is now at 16000 feet and going to 17000 feet. *RMI*-Dunn is at the fixed line.

July 3. Clear beautiful day. Lowell Thomas dropped newspapers on the way over to Camp Denali. The *Genet* group is at 17000 feet and will try for the summit when the winds are calm. *The Alpine Club of Canada (ACC),* the *Yugoslavs*, and some other parties are at 10000 feet. Mike Covington is back; we talked for about an hour before he flew out. He is now in partnership with Peter Habeler. Mike is interested in having me do a small part of a book on Denali with him. He says a lot of people are asking for this sort of thing. They plan to have worldwide climbs, plus a climbing school here. Mike used to be a musician and songwriter. He was linked with Garfunkel in England and they said he would be much happier on the Mountain, which he chose instead of a very large contract. *Way-Too-High* is at 16400 feet and going to 17000 feet tomorrow. The solo Englishman is there.

July 4. I talked to Cliff. The steaks that he sent up were never delivered to me, nor was the plastic tarp. Cliff gave specific instructions to the Swiss group to give these things to me. Cliff was pretty mad so they are going to pay for the steak. I talked to 22 in Fairbanks. He called Leslie and she gave him all the latest news. I think he has a direct line of sight to Foraker and one of the high snow fields is functioning like a huge reflector. Also, I listened to Radio Moscow today, through a series of unusual radio situations here. It's been mostly cloudy and rainy most of today.

July 5. Cliff called about the weather. NPS called with weather, which I broadcast every day. *RMI*-Dunn is at 17000 feet with 40 mile-per-hour winds gusting to 60 miles per hour *RMI*-Ershler is not in contact yet. I advised him that ten Mexicans would be in Seattle in August for about fourteen days, and might be interested in a climb of Rainier and/or a seminar. I had previously been advised that *Genet* had two sick people, but they have recovered. I also hear terrible stories about the arrogant solo Englishman who mooches from everyone. He came up to me and wanted me to cook him a hot meal, which didn't work very well for him. He came to this mountain poorly equipped and has counted on everyone taking care of him.

Now the news item: An Italian lady, solo climber is here. She also looks to be very poorly equipped and ill prepared for this Mountain. The crevasses are opening up, the snow is soft and it is very hazardous to travel alone. She is a little grey-haired lady in her 50s. She is a medical research doctor and her specialty is pain. I asked her if she had experienced a lot of pain. She looked amazed and then said she had experienced pain, so I do not know any more than I did, except my questions provoked some deep inner response, but in a defiant way.

She was arrested in the Yukon (I'm enclosing the newspaper article). It's my opinion that the Yukon Government probably saved her life, and furthermore, she ought to know whether she is in the United States or Canada. St. Elias is right on the border, but she still ought to know those basics. I do not think the NPS is out of line in their policies in requiring people to register to climb this Mountain. I've asked climbers from Communist countries what they thought and they didn't think it was out of line. One of our top climbers, after having his life saved along with that of someone he was helping on a difficult route several years ago, said he would never criticize the registration policy again or the recommendation to carry a radio.

July 6.   The Swiss left and now I am alone. What a treat! *Way-Too-High* called; they have descended to 14000 feet and are waiting to go again. Now there are whiteout conditions. The Canadians, also, are there, and the solo Englishman, plus some others lower down by Windy Corner. George, from *RMI*-Dunn, called from 17000 feet around noon. Also there, are the two other Japanese from *Black Box*, *Wendy's Wing Ding* and the *Genet* group are there. Winds are gusting to 40 miles per hour. *RMI*-Dunn will descend instead of doing the traverse as his food is low. In the evening, I could hear a Russian station on HW8 (commonly referred to as HOT WATER-8), which is my CW. I can hear all over, but cannot get out and do not know what the problem is. This is an opportunity to be up here, but how frustrating to not be able to transmit!

July 7.   Beautiful, cool, clear day. Still alone. A couple of planes flew by in the morning, the latter one headed up the Kahiltna. I do not know who it is. I would surely like to go for a ride. Talkeetna Air Taxi gave Thelma her ride in here for nothing. It costs about $225 round trip. Otherwise, I hope to be able to get over to the Wickersham Wall for some pictures, as I want to write a Spanish story about the wall, and also about this year's approach coming into the Mountain. Then I want to do a science fiction one about the invaders (the black planes and helicopters with no human life aboard, and the little animal who roams the glacier with the raven, Dotson). I finished reading a science fiction anthology, *Alone Around the World* by Naomi Jones, and am now reading *King Arthur*. Next it's *Pavorotti*, and then *Trinity*. I also keep busy with Japanese, Russian, Spanish and ham radio.

July 8. What started out as a beautiful day, turned into rain in the afternoon, and back to the usual dismal weather. I listened to WL7ARE, but could not make contact. Unusual atmospheric conditions often produce unusual radio conditions. Tonight, I talked to an FAA man in Cold Bay, Alaska, and that is quite a ways away. I am trying to get some things packed, so I can leave by the 19th or 20th. My plane won't get in until the morning of the 29th, so I could have stayed on this Mountain longer, but I may have to stay longer anyway if the weather socks in.

July 9. I heard from Roy that Carol will be on CW and will try to make contact. Later, Jay came in with a chocolate milk shake from Talkeetna. I talked to the Canadians on the West Rib. They surely are strong, as are the Yugoslavs—*Aerie Northwest* at 14000 feet. The Greeks flew in with *North Cascade* (Allan Kearney) and they can hardly speak English. I haven't seen the Italian lady. I talked to Chile and will broadcast weather in Spanish on Channel 1 at 12:05, after the English broadcast at 12:00. Alternate times are 12:15, 12:30, 12:35 and 6:00, 6:30. I need a price for ski-pole rental for the Greeks. I obtained a price from *RMI*-Dunn for summit climbs and seminars, as I received a letter from the Mexican Mountain Rescue that they will be in Seattle the second week of August.

July 10. It was clear earlier, but now there is lots of haze from forest fire in the Park. Also, there is plenty of thunder and lightning. The Norwegians did the Cassin—I like them a lot. I talked to the Canadians, and I talked to Lady Sunflower about the weather. The French and *Way-Too-High* came back. Cathy's ski pole rentals are $2 (very inexpensive). *Aerie Northwest* was at 14000 feet at 11:30 a.m., in beautiful weather, and going up. I couldn't get Anchorage weather bureau data because the line was temporarily disconnected. I did get a report from FAA Talkeetna through NPS. I talked to 22 in Fairbanks. Carol went over later to talk to me on 22's CB about problems with CW. I set up two schedules on two different frequencies. (I couldn't meet the schedules, because six climbers were in my tent.) We know some of the same climbers in Washington. Carol had a lot to say. Al, Leslie Salisbury and Roy Davies all sent "Hello." There may be interference between the 80-meter and 40-meter antennas. If the co-ax (coaxial cable) is bad, then Al suggests clipping one of the 40-meter wires and plugging it into the adapter, which then will act as a 40-meter co-ax antennae.

Al is going to try to get me on his special CB, far enough away from Fairbanks, on Chena Ridge, so that his signals are bouncing off one of the high snow fields on Mt. Foraker. It's the highest and best reflector around. McKinley is directly in the way of Fairbanks, but I can get Fairbanks NOA weather station, which I think is bounced off some snow fields on Hunter. I move a few feet in and receive NOA weather from Anchorage. Today I was receiving Code on the CB Channel 19, about the same time Radio Moscow is on. Radio work is fascinating. If you give me a birthday present, I need radio equipment. Everything I have, except my key, was collected by Carol from many of the Fairbanks "hams" before I left. They went to a lot of effort to try to get me on the air and I'm having transmitting problems, so by various means we are trying to analyze them. The weather here is much better now. Thank you for all your letters and pressed petals and I think I can make the Milwaukee date—just barely.

July 11. I talked to Sunflower Lady and KES7604 (Roy), because I believe the tower is leaning. I "righted mast" later, so will see if that affects reception and transmission to their locations. The leader of the Greek group is having a terrible time communicating. After Nick felt better, the Greek leader of the three decided to leave him. The Greek party is being led by *North Cascades'* Allan Kearney, who is a friend of mine. Late at night, or early in the morning the Chileans returned, as did the Canadians.

July 12. Today, or rather last night, I decided that my tent had to be leveled, since I still have a week to go and I might be stranded much longer with virtually no help to fix the tent. It's a sourdough type of tent, which means that it's very heavy work; so I got the help of climbers from Seattle, France and Chile. The Canadians slept through it all, but later came by. The Chileans did a fantastic job and my attitude toward them changed remarkably. The leader is a fine man and invited me to Chile. He spent several years in Mexico in various climbing areas and we discussed the problems in Mexico, or rather, the lack of problems to prepare for in expedition climbing—namely

107

adverse weather and the necessity of being together as a team for a long time under extreme stress, as one experiences here as well as in Patagonia.

Anyway, the job got done, and I had to tear down all the radio gear, put the CB into operation outside, and later, reassemble everything again—all three radios. Now I just received word from 22 in Fairbanks, and three of the best "hams" there are going to be calling tonight to try to make contact with a complicated schedule. They will call on 80 meters at 10:00 and again at 11:00, and continuously for 20 minutes after those times. I will try to transmit to them if I can. At 11:35 we will switch to 40 meters for 20 minutes with the same procedure. At 10:30 and 11:30, 22 will be on the air on CB to coordinate if needed. The efforts of these "hams," I think, equal efforts of the climbers to climb mountains. Anyway it is very interesting, so I hope I can do OK.

I think there is something wrong with the set or antennae, or it is a complicated problem with antennae interference. Reception in this area is tremendously tricky; I'm finding out more and more with HF, CB, NOA and the CW. Maybe you are not interested in all this detail about climber problems and communication, but this is the first I've had time to write much (the last couple of weeks). This is not to say I'm not busy—I am. The hours are long. The Yugoslavs should be back here soon, as will *RMI*-Ershler and *Aerie Northwest,* which will leave nineteen still trying for the summit. All the *RMI* leaders speak of Marty and we all share the loss of her. She was a great person and climber.

July 13. Today I am a new person. I made my first contact on my ham rig. At least when the Fairbanks "hams" determined that they were going to get contact here, they did. Burt used a lot of power. I was surprised when I first heard my call sign on 80 meters and then his call sign when I was listening. This was from 10:00-10:20. I transmitted until 10:25. At 10:30 I was on CB to 22. I informed Vi that I had picked up KL7LRT, but couldn't pick up KL7AG or KL7GBG. They were all trying to call at the same time, at slightly different frequencies I think, because I picked up Burt on 3731.

At 11:00 we tried again and I heard Burt (only Burt tried now) sending a message. He actually copied me in Fairbanks. His signal was weak this time, probably trying to ascertain the amount of power necessary to reach here. Again, I transmitted at 11:20 and 11:25 and then talked to 22 on the CB at 11:30. They can copy me. Then at 11:35-11:55 we tried on 40 meters and Burt is booming in loud and clear with his message. I'm so nervous I barely copy slow code, but we made contact. Then at 12 midnight, I was back on the air with 22 on CB. He told me Burt was using a tremendous amount of power. Burt, I believe, has the best set up in Fairbanks. 22 also told me that someone on Chena Hot Springs Road picks me up. Well now, it's back to work to get my code speed up so I can feel more comfortable copying code.

Later: The day is quite nice with scattered clouds; there are three Americans, two French, seven Chileans, three Yugoslavs and one Greek waiting to fly out. The French are impatient and complain about how the Swiss are the best pilots. They want me to give them my opinion of all pilots (who are my bosses and friends), which I won't do and then they talk about how their own pilot isn't as courageous as some others. Doug landed the other day in fog, which is about the most frightening thing I've ever seen. He took off in a whiteout without passengers, after I had three people ready to fly out, because it was too dangerous. And then the French talked about Jim who turned around down on the glacier, approximately 15 miles away when he couldn't get above or below the clouds. Wow, some of these climbers! I really have to contain my temper. These pilots we have here are some of the best in the world and some of these climbers have called them "sunshine pilots."

Later: Everyone flew out, but one solo flew in. The glacier is in terrible condition, excessively dangerous. Tonight I will work with Carol on code starting at 11:40 until midnight. She will use Burt's station. He signs on, because Burt is an extra and Carol is an advanced. There are five licenses starting with novice, and proceeding through technician, general, advanced and extra.

July 14.   All alone on my birthday, but then the NPS sang "Happy Birthday" on the radio. Then Jim was trying to fly in and said "Happy Birthday." Then Lowell flew over and said Cliff said it was my birthday, so he said "Happy Birthday" from high overhead. Then Billie (Lady Sunflower) called up and said "Happy Birthday." After that *Aerie Northwest* came in and one climber had a wrist watch that played "Happy Birthday." So I had an unusual birthday and a very nice one. The weather has turned bad again.

Carsten's Ridge, along the Muldrow Glacier route.

Chapter Eight — 1983

Death in a crevasse —
a tragedy assessed

May 18. I left for Talkeetna after stopping by the office, which was having a party. I had a piece of pizza and a strawberry, and left. About thirty miles out of Cantinell, the car lost power and I barely made it into Cantinell. It took four hours and eighty-five dollars to find out that the exhaust pipe had collapsed, so I drove minus muffler and tail pipe to Talkeetna.

May 19. Lowell and I took off for the Mountain, but conditions were too bad, so we went back to have supper and then tried again. It was a real spooky flight, in amongst the peaks of Hunter and Foraker, with the wind being very gusty, and it was also cloudy. It was a beautiful flight, but spooky, so we headed to Anchorage. Lowell had previously called his wife there, who called Anne and said we might not be able to fly in. So I ended up at Anne's. Carl was in Germany. We had a nice chat.

May 20. Lowell called about 6:40 a.m. So off we went to the Mountain. This time we got in, but the winds were pretty bad. This has lasted most of the day with excessively high winds above. Then, the radio started acting up and the telephone wouldn't work. The generator didn't function correctly and the battery was down, so I went to work. I started out with major problems in communications. All that works now is my ham set, which I set up, and my weather radio. Cliff took the generator out. The weather doesn't look very good. There are very few foreign climbers this year as compared to other years.

May 21. Lowell Thomas got in. The weather is not good. I sent out a message for someone to monitor 3735 at 8:00-9:30 p.m. and later picked up KL7JKW at Montana Creek. Earlier several flights came in and went out, but the winds are very bad, and it's cloudy.

May 22. Lowell Thomas tried to get up to 14000 feet, but conditions would not allow it. He landed here and took out one person. Later, Tony came in and took out three. He did not bring the generator. I talked to KL7JKW on CW. It was 50 degrees and raining in Montana Creek. Then along came Lowell Thomas and a chopper heading to a higher elevation on the Mountain. I can copy here with a hand held set, but they cannot transmit from 14000 feet. Somebody higher on the Mountain has a broken leg. I do not know the extent of the problems, nor the party, nor its location, but it is higher than 14000 feet. The pilot could not land with the down draft there, so the rescue party will have to move the injured person up to the saddle (wherever that is). So, they picked up two frostbite victims at 14000 feet and went back. It surely is a handicap not to have communication here. There could be terrible problems here and the only link I would have is with one CB hand-held set, which is only good if a plane flies over, or if I walk for fifteen minutes up the glacier into an avalanche area and then try to contact 14000 feet from there. Besides, they frequently are not on the air up there, even though they are staffed with solar panels, telephone and radios, and probably six to eight people. Here, all I have is myself and one sure communication with my ham rig. The big battery is down and I have no generator. Talkeetna Air Taxi should have gotten a generator in today, which is more important than bringing in clients!

May 23. We have about one inch of new snow. Cloudy, partial clearing. I made contact with KL7JKW at 10:00 a.m. and gave the weather from here for relay to NPS. Then Lowell Thomas came along and also a chopper. There is a problem at 17200 or 17300 feet with at least a broken leg. The chopper was having a difficult time landing, and it is low on fuel. No contact from here with the hand-held set. I could only partially monitor some of what was going on. By 11:00 I had not seen the chopper or 19V leave, and I do not know the status. I will try to contact KL7JKW this evening. NOA weather reports indicate a continuation of clouds and possible/probable showers on the lower and upper Susitna. There are several fronts to the west in the Dutch Harbor area and in the southeast. To the north the Tenana valley has better conditions today, but they are probably worsening. I talked a lot to the *Hollander-Aerie* party and to a member of the *ACC* who did the Muldrow-Kahiltna Traverse. Weather is very poor by now and there are now nine waiting for Talkeetna Air Taxi, and seven for K-2, and none for Hudson. One man from *ACC* helped me put small batteries together for power for a tape deck.

May 24. The weather cleared at 4:00 a.m. Lowell Thomas and the chopper came through. Later, about 6:00 a.m., Talkeetna Air Taxi started to fly, followed by K-2 with fifty people to fly out.

May 25. The generator does not work again. NBC came in with Doug to film. I had an interview with NBC and played my violin for them; they also taped Doug, two others and me on communications. Cliff is trying to call. Lady Sunflower picked up the call. I advised that Doug took out the generator. The telephone needs more power, and power is limited on the CB. Two ladies from Missoula were here and flew out. I told them my mother had lived in Missoula and went to the university and liked Montana. Two of their party went on and over to climb Foraker. All had been up the Mountain. Eight o'clock contact with KL7JKW at Montana Creek. Later, eight from *RMI* came back. The leader is Pete Whittaker, who is the son of either Jim or Lou—Jim, I think. Also, three Germans are back. The Japanese arrived and gave me two photos taken three years ago (Japanese Railroad Workers.)

May 26. Weather will probably clear here. It snowed two inches last night. Please advise Fred Healy that I talk to KL7JKW on 3735. I will write to Fred. The telephone number here is 907-733-2525. I am on an eleven-party line. Please do not say any gossip or personal matters, if you should call me. Also, phone is out of commission a lot. Limit calls to three to five minutes. Lowell saw Georgia TV from last year in Hawaii. Try to call once per week. The generator is not charging the battery. I got one massage through to Lady Sunflower, and the power is about all gone. I talked to Montana Creek KL7JKW about pertinent information. Fifty-five climbers flew out and twenty-one flew in. John Svenson flew out. (Again, my phone number is 907-733-2525).

May 27. Doug brought in the generator and I now have a battery from Jim. Cliff also brought one in as a back-up. The big one is being charged down in Talkeetna. Nancy Simmerman called from K-2 and wanted to come up, as she is doing a large portfolio book of photos for Alaska. I may be in that book. Also, my contact in Montana Creek on ham rig, told me last night that I was on TV (NBC, Channel 2). Nancy flew in and she had lived in Fairbanks quite awhile so we had a pleasant chat about various acquaintances.

May 28.   Nancy took a lot of photos of me and the area and the climbers that were here. Nic and Char are back, but we didn't have much time to chat. Both will be back soon. We will probably have another opportunity. They were married last fall and are good friends of mine. They are guides. Mike Covington will soon be back, as will Gary Bocarde, Steve Gall, John Svenson and Peter Habeler. Weather closed in by the evening.

The prediction for the weekend is not good. There are two climbers on Hunter on an extreme route, and a team of Hollanders on the standard route, which is treacherous right now with the bad snow conditions. The problem is the warm weather we had in April, which was followed by colder weather and continued snowfall now. The result is varying layers of different types of snow, which are conducive to avalanche conditions.

May 29.   The weather is grim with snow and poor visibility. I just got through talking to you and assume I'll receive mail as soon as they can fly again. Also, I'll have the battery charged up before talking, rather than doing it afterwards, as I am now. It is great to have communications back and I'm certainly glad I'm a ham for emergencies, because code can get through when voice can not, and from about anywhere. I have my code tapes, so I also practice code. I must study Japanese now.

Besides the two Hunter parties, which are on very difficult routes, there are two Japanese parties. One, a group of five, is doing the West Buttress; and the other (two) is training on the West Buttress and then will go over to do the American Direct. This is one of the most exposed and difficult routes on the Mountain and the avalanche danger is terrible. We have never seen again several of the parties who have gone up the Northeast Fork of the Kahiltna to attempt the American Direct or other routes in that area.

People Magazine wanted to have an interview with me, but I couldn't call them back, as I was on the Mountain with no communications, so by next Tuesday they may not be interested. I talked to Lowell on his third attempt to get in here; and I can't remember whether I mentioned that in my first letter or not. Besides you haven't received it yet, so I mention it again.

I'm reading *One Hundred Years of Solitude* by Garcia Marquez; the title, at least, is appropriate reading for up here. I have a lot to do with my own work plus whatever goes on here. There are not so many climbers on the Mountain now, but the conditions do not look at all good. Oh yes, Lowell brought me some tomatoes, lettuce, sprouts, grapefruit, one white onion, (they came from Anchorage) and also a bunch of newspapers. Nancy brought me a box of strawberries and Cliff brought me a chicken, so my menus have been pretty good lately.

May 30. The winds are picking up and they are roaring overhead, so it looks like the Mountain is in for some genuine weather. Five of the Hollanders came back to Kahiltna Base for a short visit and tea in the New Zealander's tent. The avalanches and snow conditions make climbing on their route terrible. There are some climbers on the Cassin and two on the Northwest Buttress of Hunter, which, with these snow conditions and avalanches and winds, are pretty grim.

May 31. The storm has let up for a short time today so they may be able to fly—at least they'll try. Fairbanks hit a record of 100 degrees day before yesterday; fires in the interior, a cold air mass moved in from the northwest and the wet weather came in from the south. Consequently, the weather was not calm. A flock of little birds got lost in the storm, very few survived. I fed two in my tent, but one died anyway. Otherwise, things are OK.

June 1. The weather is terrible. It rained all night with high winds. Up higher it must be unbelievable. I do not know when this will subside. Now it is snowing and the winds have shifted to northwest, so colder air is moving in. I talked to Roger at NPS about climbing parties and the weather, and that the battery will not take a good charge. Vern Tajas and Schmidt came in late. They just did the Cassin. *West Point* (three) left. The weather got worse and planes couldn't fly. After I took out the small light they had wired in parallel on the generator, the battery began to take a charge rather than discharge. Joe Horiskey of *RMI* talked quite awhile about Rainier and the trash problem in the mountains and particularly the heavily-used ones like Rainier and McKinley.

June 2. Tony and Doug of Talkeetna Air Taxi and Jim of K-2 came in to pick up climbers. Talkeetna Air Taxi had four and took one of Hudson's also. Tony, who works for Doug, took the gear, while Doug just took passengers. Vern preferred to ride with Jim and K-2 was in. Weather started to move in and in the storm that followed, Mark Oswald, of *Klockwork*, came in alone from Kahiltna Pass. Waterman, of NPS, was at 14000 feet; he breathes hard when talking on the radio—can't shake the cold and also is spitting up blood. I hear that I'm to get a weatherport, which will certainly be better accommodation.

I talked to *West Point* at 5:30 p.m. At 8:00 p.m., I made good contact on sked with KL7JKW and then atmospheric conditions became terrible. The signals faded in and out about as fast as dits and dots. After that the CB had some of the weirdest noises. Living with radio noise, particularly at night, is as eerie as any science fiction story.

June 3. Winds are calm, but it snowed about a foot of new last night; temperature is 32 degrees. I called Bob Beaver of *People Magazine*, as he had wanted some sort of interview before I left, but I didn't have time to talk, and then communications were knocked out. By now he doesn't work for *People* anymore, so don't look for me in *People*. I talked to the two Japanese for one and one-half hours who are going to do the American Direct Ascent.

Later: This eleven-party line I'm on must be one of the weirdest in the world. It starts at (1) 14000 feet with the doctors and their consultations, and one who is a lady's man, and their weather; then (2) 7500 feet here with critical landing problems, battery and generator problems, location and condition of climbers and conferences between 14000 feet, here and NPS, and then (3) the Bush. There are the airplane problems of landing on the lakes, who is planting what in their garden, the mosquitoes and the float plane, which is about totaled from an unsuccessful take-off in too small a lake, which everyone is trying to keep quiet because it's a local pilot (and it is not Cliff); and the grandfather who is mad at his grand-daughter who left him in Anchorage and took the keys to the car with her when she went back to the Bush; he finally got some keys today, but then got a flat, etc.

Now I must do code with KL7JKW and I plan on writing to Fred. Maybe we can make contact some Monday on 15 meters when the band is in. I surely hope so.

I just finished reading *100 Anos de Soledad* por Gabriel Garcia Marquez and *Fables and Fairy Tails* by Leo Tolstoy. I think that Tolstoy's equals, if not surpasses, *Anderson and Grimm's Fairy Tales*. I'm now reading *El Hallo de Oro* por Juan Rulfo, *First Love and Other Tales* by Ivan Turgenev, *Vuelta* por Octavio Paz, *The Labyrinth of Solitude* by Octavio Paz and *Labyrinth* by Jorge Borges.

I'm trying to speed up my code, so I practice daily, plus I'm keeping my schedule with Del at Montana Creek. I'm also doing Japanese, which is essential with the two that are going on the American Direct, and expect to start practicing my violin. I hope the weatherport comes in soon, so I can get things arranged before I have to think about leaving. I planted my lettuce seeds. Happy Father's Day!

June 4. I got two Japanese and one young man, who had slight pulmonary edema, to work on the landing strip which had over one and one half feet of snow. One New Zealander did nothing and the other New Zealander did a little work with lots of complaints, after I asked both of them three times. They said they land in seaplanes in New Zealand. Klewin and Bibler walked in from the lower Kahiltna. They did a new route up the Northwest Buttress of Hunter and spent six nights on top before they could see to come down the West Ridge. They were short on food, but ran into the Hollanders who gave them some food, and they came back here OK.

John Quimby, who was here last year with the Medics, came down from 14000 feet and we both hope he can come back to help put up the new weatherport, which will be a vast improvement in living and working conditions. Some lady on the party line was mad, as usual, about the way we use our phones, and complained to the service man. (Presumably this lady considered the rescue of climbers with broken legs or high altitude sickness of much less importance than the following "soap opera".)

"Grandma, recently widowed, is coming up from Arkansas with her son and daughter-in-law, plus a large dog, all riding in their car with a huge trailer that they are pulling. They got caught in Missouri without the proper overload trailer springs. Regardless of spring problems they hope to get to South Dakota by tomorrow night."

June 5. Today was busy. It started around 5:00 a.m., and they started flying. Thirty-eight flew in and ten flew out. Fortunately, by the time you called, things had calmed down. During the rush, I heard part of the saga:

"They got caught in a rain storm and got all wet in the middle of the night and finally had to eat in a restaurant. This was a big crisis."

Then that's all I heard. The phone didn't work for a long

time and everyone blamed it on the camp at 14000 feet. Finally the problem was found in the repeater on Bald Mountain.

I talked to the Basques, who do not know English, and they seemed so happy to find someone to talk to them. They are friends of one of the Basques that I talked to quite a lot last year. They said they had seen many pictures of this, but they could not believe the magnitude and beauty of it. I talked to *Miyuksi* (Nupiak word for climber) at base of Foraker. They will do the southeast ridge. One Japanese in the group of five has HAPE (high altitude pulmonary edema) at 14000 feet. Friends of Roy Davies flew in with Doug to see the Kahiltna Glacier. They were from Florida. Roy and Bonnie plan to move down there. I hope Roy is able to get up here before he and Bonnie leave.

The Japanese team, *Sangakudoshikai* (2) moved to Camp One on the east fork of the Kahiltna to do the American Direct route.

June 6.   Very windy and very unusual wind storms this year. There is a storm off the northwest coast of Alaska with cyclonic winds. *Miyuksi* is going to go to 9000 feet today.

"Grandma and family are in Sioux Falls with voltage regulator or alternator problems, plus one or two new tires and shocks and springs."

Traleika-Maku is back.

June 7.   Ned Lewis and Stacy Taneguchi came back from the Lowe-Kennedy route on Hunter. Snow and ice conditions are terrible, just mush under a crust, prime avalanche problems. I talked to *Miyuksi* on Foraker.

June 8.   *Sangakudoshikai*, at 14000 feet, is about to climb toward 16000 feet. The *Bernafat* group came back, one flew out. They are from France, and were here last year. Mrs. Bernafat gave me a bottle of French perfume.

June 9.   I heard there was a bad problem with a Reeves plane out by Cold Bay in the Aleutians. It lost a propeller, but got back. The *Japanese Glacier Alpine Club* is still at 14000 feet. Stacy and Ned Lewis are at the base of the West Kahiltna. Rolf Gruage is at 17000 feet with severe frostbite; according to John Waterman of NPS, he has frozen and thawed his feet many times in the last six or seven days. He needs evacuation. A rescue party brought him down to 14000 feet. Tomorrow they will make an airstrip for Lowell Thomas to land at 14000 feet. *Sangakudoshikai* called in the evening. They are at 16000 feet.

Denali Blue Zenith will go for the summit tomorrow; they wanted to send a personal message to friends. I advised that they should decide to what extent they wanted the message to be heard, as they had a huge audience on the radio and telephone.

"Grandma is about two days outside of Dawson, and the family feud goes on with the grand-daughter. After Grandma is through with any of her families' spouses, it will be a wonder of the world if any of their marriages survive." Today it is cold and windy.

June 10.   The winds died down during the night and it was a beautiful day, but cold in the morning. I talked to *Sangakudoshikai* at 14600 feet. They hope to go to the top today, but it is unlikely, as they have the most important and difficult part of the American Direct Ascent route to do today. Lowell Thomas flew to 14000 feet and evacuated Gruage and his climbing partner from there. This year he has a supercharger, which gives him a lot more climbing rate of ascent and high altitude capability. John Q. called from Anchorage and said he had found the battery that I wanted.

"Grandma called from Sasketoon, Canada, and the family here is beginning to feel the teeth of Grandma who is running up terrible phone bills and the people here are not very rich."

Later: I discovered that Doug Geeting's tent was missing; either the wind carried it off or someone lifted it. It was a good custom-made tent that he left here in case he got stranded on the glacier. Therefore I had to get in touch with all the tent companies and NPS about this problem and check lists of who came in and flew out in the last couple of days.

At 5:00 p.m., approximately, I received a call from the *Japanese Glacier Alpine Club* in a state of duress. They told me they needed rescue, and that's one word in Japanese I can't forget. They cannot move and are in the area of 19000 feet. I got hold of Yamakami and together we found out that one (Chiba) has a broken leg, and one (Watanabe) has a broken arm. Mike Covington is coming back to fly out. The rest of his team went with one of his other guides up the West Buttress to the Ruth Glacier. They were going to do another route via the Ruth. The snow and ice are in terrible condition. Mike is the guide who sent me the tent last year.

By now, everyone is in contact about the problems up above. The leader, Yamakami, had pulmonary edema at 14000 feet.

119

At 14000 feet, a team got together and started for 17000 feet. Chiba and Watanabe have one day of food, one stove, clothes and a yellow bivouac tent. Blue sky and no wind up there. They are lucky. The rescue party, including Peter Hackett and Brian Okonek, is to arrive at 9:00 p.m. at 17000 feet. I talked to Bob Gerhard on the phone about a rescue for the Japanese. I also tried to get in touch with *Denali Blue Zenith*, as they are in the general area. I was unable to make contact with *Sangakudoshikai* at the usual time.

The rescue party arrived at 17000 feet at 8:40 p.m., and now the two Japanese who were at 17000 feet can talk to Chiba and Watanabe at 19000 feet. We scheduled to talk to the Japanese at 19000 feet, from here, every half hour, and to be in continuous contact with 17000 feet, 14000 feet and NPS, Talkeetna. As the night wears on, the injured Japanese are getting cold and it is imperative that they keep together and keep as warm as possible. I advised them to melt water and keep fluids down. Every half hour I talk to the Japanese. Yamakami spent all night beside the radio. We drink tea and eat some celery. Yamakami must feel terribly bad, because he is their leader and he came down with pulmonary edema so badly at 14000 feet that only oxygen there saved his life.

At 12:50 a.m. the rescue party reached the injured. Chiba has a severe knee injury and Watanabe has what appears to be a chest injury. It does not look as serious as it first appeared to be. The rescuers worked their way down with Chiba, and arrived at 17000 feet totally exhausted, as this is their second rescue in a couple of days. After rescuers have rested, they will talk about a procedure to get the Japanese to 14000 feet, or to have them evacuated by helicopter. I heard from *Denali Blue Zenith* that they had bivouacked at 19000 feet, but had never seen the Japanese.

The two well-known climbers *Sangakudoshikai* have made probably the third ascent of the American Direct Ascent, in record time, and are offering any assistance they can in helping the other Japanese team. Later, the *Miyuksi* team called about one person with a sore throat—I phoned Peter Hackett, and their antibiotic and dosages are OK.

"Grandma and family are not in Dawson Creek, and she has to have medicine as she is sick. Grandma has charged $800 worth of telephone bills."

June 12. Calm and overcast clouds lifting over the lower Kahiltna. The rescue party will move Chiba down to 14000 feet. It took about ten hours. They lowered him down Rescue Gulch. West Point came back and flew out. Roy is to be a lawyer and was upset with his two team members who were studying to be mechanical and electrical engineers, I think.

Call from 14000 feet: Steve Gall, at 11000 feet needs gear and Mike Harr probably will bring down Will Wolfrom, a pulmonary edema victim, to fly out. Three strong Brits are going to bring oxygen. When Will Wolfrom came in, he was in bad shape, could hardly walk, and flew out immediately. *Miyuksi* (Nupiak, meaning climber) was just on top of Foraker and on the way down.

June 13. *Miyuksi* is at high camp. The oxygen tank, which I sent to Talkeetna last night, never got on board Lowell Thomas' plane, as he did not stop in Talkeetna. He is to go to 14000 feet to pick up one person (bad frostbite, skin sluffing off) and directly to Providence. Later in the day, Monty Graham showed up from Hunter with Beecher. Monty has an eye problem; the pupil on his right eye is smaller than the left. The right side of his face is puffy, he can not focus on distant objects or distinguish color with his right eye, and sees two images. He discovered the problem when he tried to focus a camera. His left eye is OK, but is starting to blur. I called Peter Hackett and described the symptoms. It does not sound like snow blindness and Peter advised medical attention. They went back to the base of Hunter and wanted to go down glacier to do some more climbing. If his condition does not improve, they will come back here tomorrow. University of Montana people came in to climb. One of the *Hollanders* has a foot injury.

June 14. Snowing lightly. I'm delivering messages back and forth between Ralph, with the *Miyuksi* party, and Susan, his wife in Talkeetna. I talked to NPS about the weatherport tent to come in. *Miyuksi* experienced 40 mile-per-hour winds out of the southwest in the last twelve hours. Relayed *Miyuksi* messages. Relayed message from Ralph to Susan. K-2 is now varnishing the floor for the weatherport. 5:22 p.m. *Miyuksi* is now at 13800 feet with winds up to 30 miles per hour, and digging a snow cave. The *Beecher-Graham* party, which had been on Hunter, advised that one *Hollander* would stay behind at the foot of Foraker, while the other three try to climb. *Aerie*

Northwest has gone up. *Denali Blue Zenith* and two others from the original *Hollander-Hunter* group are climbing.

June 15. *The Ridge Riders* on the Cassin are at 15000 feet; they took one and one half days off to rest and are dug in below a rock band. It is clear with no wind and little precipitation. Art Mannix of *Genet Expeditions* called from 17000 feet. *ECP* had arrived at 14000 feet and solo Saunders is coming up. Cliff called about *Sangakudoshikai* as they had wanted to fly out today. The weather is not flyable. NPS weather bureau advises of a big front moving in from the Bering Sea. Solo climber, Helmut, is to come in. *Ridge Riders* are now at 200 feet below the first rock band and it is 10 degrees with light snow. Stolpman is at 14000 feet.

June 16. There are four inches of new wet snow accumulated, and a little blue overhead. *Miyuski* called from Foraker. They have one and one half days of food left with half rations, and fuel for about three more days. They are camped about 12000 feet at the double rocks, and have about 1000 feet of 45-degree slope to descend in about a foot of powder, hopefully they can kick it off as they descend. 7:25: *Miyuksi* called again and asked about the *Hollanders*. I advised them that I didn't know their whereabouts except that two would ascend, and one was remaining below with a bad foot. 7:32: NPS advises that weather might improve before it gets worse. 7:45: In a whiteout here. *Miyuksi* advises that they will descend and put in good anchors. 9:11: Doug is trying to come in with the Harry Johnson party. They have tons of food and gear.

This weather that Doug is trying to land in is awful. *Ridge Riders* are at 15000 feet; it's clear and no wind, as so often occurs on the south face routes, but not always. Lowell Thomas reports that one lone climber is coming across the glacier from Foraker to Hunter. 12:01: I talked to Lowell Thomas, really down to deck here. I talked to Lady Sunflower, it's raining like crazy there and everything looks black towards the Mountain. Cliff called about the weather. 12:53: Called K-2 and Talkeetna Air Taxi about the weather: lots of blue, big bands of clouds by Foraker. 3:05: Cliff called about his clients; he forgot to bring the rainbow trout. *Prairie Ramblers* are at 17000 feet. 7:20: *Miyuksi* is at 10400 feet and plan to go to 8500 feet tonight. Harry Johnson was taking a sled without asking; I explained the policy of asking first, because I had a tally sheet of equipment and gear and fuel for the climbers and pilots. They said

122

that Doug had told them to grab some sleds. I again affirmed that I needed to know what was left and what was going out. John Svenson is at 16000 feet.

June 17. I called NPS about gasoline for the generator. I advised them that Al Kearny, leader of *North Cascades (American Alpine Institute)*, and Tom Kairney are returning to Kahiltna Base with pulmonary edema. Called Doug about the sleds; he will bring some more. We also talked about people to come out, and I advised him that Alan Kearny of K-2 and Tom Kairney of Hudson, both have pulmonary edema and are coming down. Doug said to let him know when they arrive, and he'll come get them—this is crazy! I called Cliff to tell him that his client, Tom is back, and said Doug would like to pick him up. Alan Kearny wants to stay to see if he improves. Cliff came in with salmon and rainbow trout and picked up his own client. *Miyuksi* is at 8500 feet and going to descend to their camp late in the afternoon on the southwest fork. I called Talkeetna Air Taxi: if it is too slushy on the southwest fork, they'll have to come to the Kahiltna southeast fork; otherwise they should turn on their CB for pick-up. Julie of K-2 called about sightseers. I contacted Jim in the air. *North Cascades* is at 17200 feet. Stolpman is at 16400 feet. John Svenson is at 17000 feet.

The Taiwanese (nine) arrived today, and what a nice group. I surely hope they got along OK. Dick Bass and Frank Wells (who resigned his job as president of Warner Brothers for one year) are climbing seven mountains in one year and those mountains will be the tallest or highest on each continent (though, Frank will not have Everest). They may take Susan Butcher with them to the Antarctic. Susan has come in second in the Iditarod and it was really so good to see her and her dogs here in 1979. The dogs are used to riding in bush planes and are very well mannered. As the plane comes in, it is quite a sight to see all those ears pointed up. I helped to handle the dogs. The *RMI* leader of the group was Phil Ershler, who is a friend of mine. Phil had just come from Everest and is going to Peru next. Frank Wells came in and talked to me for quite awhile, and watch the operations here at Kahiltna Base. He was astounded at the amount of activity that I have and am responsible for. I liked Frank and he said he wanted to find out what else I did. I told him I always wanted to find out what a president of a movie company was like, particularly since, over a fifteen-year period, I'd only seen two movies.

Dick Bass, the oil man, knows Pat Chamey's mother who is also "oil people." Pat was one of our McKinley climbers who later died on Rainier. Dick Bass was supposed to call her two years ago when he was here to climb with Marty Hoey (my friend who was killed on Everest). Well, after bargaining and haggling with a new local restaurant for dinner for the Ershler-Bass-Wells people, Wells offered overtime plus fifteen percent, and finally I got the help at the restaurant to agree to stay and fix dinner for their group. Bass was already in Talkeetna and I called him so he could expedite from that end. Wells told me I'd have this grandiose dinner when I got back to Talkeetna, which would be steak, lobster, etc, etc. The bill for this dinner came to over $1000 for the group, or so Doug told me.

Kitty offered to take me out on a float plane trip when I get down, which would be great. Kitty was recently hired by K-2 and she used to fly here. She is a good pilot and very popular.

Tony took me out for a ride the other night to look at the Wickersham Wall. This was very interesting and I hope my pictures turned out OK. I love to fly and I've wanted to get some pictures of the Wickersham Wall for a long time. These weren't what I was really wanting, but I got to see the rock strata very close and part of the southwest routes, which was interesting and very worthwhile. The rock is a mess or mixture of the black rock, which is typical of the north peak, and the brownish rock, which is typical of the south peak. Under McKinley lie two faults, and one, I believe, is between the north and south peak.

Oh, Yes! The Taiwanese told me that at about the same time that the bad earthquake occurred in El Salvador a few days ago, they'd had a similar one in Taiwan. Now I'm invited to visit Taiwan. Lowell has been air dropping some of the newspapers. The last one landed close to a huge hole, so we took a rope, and Marty, who was along with Roger on the NPS patrol, roped up to retrieve it while Susan belayed. I had met Marty and his brother two years ago when they were trying to do Foraker and we all ended up waiting ten days for the weather to clear. Lowell's wife has been sending fresh lettuce, herbs from her herb garden (wow, are they nice) and spearmint—what a treat. Lowell is filming some things and I'm in something or other, which should eventually end up in some TV special. The wind is coming up and roaring overhead.

July 11. I had a long talk with the team that pulled the lady out of the crevasse. Her death was the most hideous, I believe, ever on this Mountain, and the circumstances are as grim as possible. It still has not been in the papers.

In the meantime, a Japanese team of two has been yo-yoing up and down the Mountain between 10000 feet, 14000 feet and 17000 feet, together or separate, but mostly separate. One has been sick and the other member has been leaving his buddy or his buddy has been going lower to feel better. Yesterday they finally were together again at 14000 feet and proceeded to 17000 feet arriving at 6:00 p.m. Today in an approaching weather front, they took off for the summit. They called from the summit at 3:28 p.m., and were descending immediately. I asked them to call when they got to 17000 feet. So far no word and it's now July 12, 12:45 a.m. as I write this. Once again, as last night, the radio is on all night. I sort of half sleep—and people ask me what I do here, and how it must be wonderful to spend my vacation here.

July 11-12. This is the story, in part, of the death of the *Sierra Club* lady, according to my notes and as told to me by Mark of the two-member *Light is Right* group. They came upon a group of people whom they had seen in the distance, and, as they moved toward them, it appeared that the group was stopped. When they arrived, the people were all sitting or standing around and *Light is Right* was informed that a lady or someone was down in a crevasse, but everything was OK (and she was warmer down there).

Mark and his partner got busy. Mark went down in the crevasse, some 40 feet down, and the lady was on top of her sled, but badly wedged in the ice with terrible head injuries and very obviously dead, since she was all blue. Mark, with a lot of effort, extracted her body and then he and Tom, his buddy, got her out. For an hour they tried with the help of Delores (*Sierra Club* member) who had rescue training to give her mouth-to-mouth resuscitation, although they knew it was hopeless. They felt the effort was necessary for the benefit of the Sierra group. (It was at this point, I believe, that the Basque climber had come along and had raced back to Kahiltna Base to tell me that the person was not breathing and that the rescue people were giving CPR).

The accident had occurred around 11:00 p.m. on June 20, 1983, and she had been in the crevasse well over an hour before *Light is Right* came along. At some point, one of the Sierra members tried to help out and fell into the crevasse, also. The lady was still alive because she said she needed help. Both her pack and sled were pulling her over backward with almost the total weight. The group made no effort to immediately relieve that pressure on her body. She had fallen about 15 feet over a lip. They had not anchored the rope to her body, nor relieved the pressure of the pack and sled, nor had they put an ice axe under the climbing rope to prevent her rope from going deeper into the lip, and thereby making rescue more difficult.

With this set of circumstances, they attempted to raise her body, sled and pack all together with all that weight on her. Eventually her climbing harness was broken. At some point now the sled (which will withstand a tremendous strain and had not been correctly attached to her pack or climbing rope in the first place) was severed from her body. At this point it may have gotten on top of her (or perhaps it had on her initial fall of 15 feet). After all of this she fell to a depth of 40 feet in the crevasse. At that point, it is generally felt, she was already dead, either from freezing (that's what *Light is Right* thought), or from a broken neck due probably to the sled (according to the autopsy), or from suffocation due to the terrible strain on her body from her pack and sled, and followed by the effort to haul her out below the lip of the crevasse, which proved impossible (according to some sources). Just before we lifted her body into the plane, her husband was blaming her death on himself, and saying he should have released the tension on her body instead of holding her in a tight ice axe arrest for so long.

The whole thing probably could have been prevented had the group known or studied crevasse rescue, and were not contemptuous of what they were told was a very difficult mountain.

The attitude of those who decided to climb anyway after the accident was not too much improved or modified. For example, five members of their group left one at 16000 feet on an extremely exposed ridge while they went on to 17000 feet. *Light is Right* came across this one member (Larry Gendroux) who said he was resting and waiting for better weather. This was on a ridge where the weather can change in seconds from calm to winds of 100-200 miles per hour. On the day of their climb, another member became ill at some (unknown to me) altitude, and went back to 17000 feet by himself. This was their assistant leader who had taken over leadership (after the leader left to accompany his wife's body back to Los Angeles). I talked to Ron, the assistant leader, on the radio when he called to advise of progress, and told him to be sure to take plenty of liquids. Finally the summit teams returned to 17000 feet and advised today that they were descending to 14000 feet. Another group, *China Lake*, a rescue group from Canada, were on the summit attempt yesterday. At one time (two days ago), their team was split and two members were in the vicinity of one single Sierra Club member, though not with him.

I have only a few days left on the Mountain, provided the weather allows me to fly off on schedule. I am happy to be going down, but I really will miss my home on the Mountain. Few in this entire world have a home like mine, with Mt. McKinley out of my back window, Mt. Hunter rising 7000 feet above the glacier (14000 feet) and about one half mile away, and Mt. Foraker five-eighths of a mile away and rising to 12000 feet above the glacier to 17000 feet. As I write, I'm listening to Mozart's "Symphonia Concertante," and an occasional avalanche. The night is beautiful with the clouds blowing around Foraker and the Foraker-Crosson Traverse.

Since Frances had a telephone at the base camp during the season of 1983 she called home about once a week and did not write so many letters home. On June 19 she called to wish her Father "Happy Father's Day." She has given a copy of "Alaska" for his present as well as my Mother's Day present. On June 26 she called to say she would be coming home by the 16th. On July 10 she called in the early evening and said she was supposed to get down from the glacier on July 14, her birthday. On July 17 she called from her home at College and said she had driven from Talkeetna.

Author takes second in her class in 1970 Fairbanks Marathon.

Epilogue

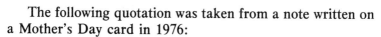

"Twilight and evening bell,
*   And after that the dark!*
And may there be no sadness of farewell,
*   When I embark!"*
Alfred Lord Tennyson

The following quotation was taken from a note written on a Mother's Day card in 1976:

"I was saddened to hear about Dr. Gehring. I didn't know him well, but I've talked to him on the phone and I know he was a good doctor and a good friend. Losses are awfully hard to take and understand. But I think that friends in time of need turn up where you least expect them. A friend may be a person, a dog, a beautiful tree or flower, the sky, a child's eyes, beautiful music. Who knows?"

"Frances meant a great deal to me as a friend, even in the short time we were together. The depth of our understanding perhaps wasn't even realized by Frances in her dear humility. But on the other hand, she opened herself to me those last few times we were together and I found a beautiful, courageous and rarely precious human being looking squarely at the path before her, afraid, but with her head up, and even daring to laugh."
Camilla Wicks, Ann Arbor, Michigan.

"Frances was an intellectual who turned her back on the Ivory Castle and embraced the world."
Carol Carnahan, Concrete, Washington

"My name is Nobuyoshi Chiba and I am the climber whom your daughter helped in Mt. McKinley in 1983. I am terribly sorry and sad to learn that Frances died from cancer and still cannot believe. One of the Japanese climber's magazines reported her death and a lot of climbers who knew Frances is very sad about the sad news like me. I recall myself in Mt.

129

McKinley when I broke my right leg waiting a rescue people. I was upset at 19000 feet in height. But Frances, the only person who could communicate with me in Japanese in Camp on Kahiltna Glacier, was a big help. Though I could read your letter with a dictionary, I could not write you for long time. With some help from a friend finally I can express my admiration of that you are publishing a book instead of Frances, please do so. With warmest memories of Frances.

Nobuyoshi Chiba, Tokyo, Japan.

"On behalf of the members of Mexican Mountain Rescue, we express our deep sorrow of Frances Randall, the Angel of Mt. McKinley."

Manuel Araiza A., Mexico City, Mexico

"Everyone at home, even the birds and the dogs, knows our sorrow about Frances. Nobody can believe it, but this is the way for all, and one day it will be our turn, don't you think? For me it is very impossible to believe she is not here anymore. May the Lord be with the Angel in Mt. McKinley for all the mountaineers without colors or way to think about the Lord. She was love for everyone in any country."

Consuelo Herrera, Mexico City

"We are grieved by the loss of our great friend. She was a good friend, and loyal to us and a great many people. She was well liked. She also has many friends in Northway area. I visited with her before she went to New York, also called her and talked with her. She was very brave. She was all smiles and cheery. She's going to be very much missed by me and all her friends. She was a wonderful person and a good friend."

Sherry Barnes, Fairbanks, Alaska

"There was something special about Frances that no one else has. I will remember her always."

Lilly Heinrich, Dryden, Washington

"Frances gave me my first pair of skis. Little did I know then the joy that would come later on in life. When I took up downhill and cross-country skiing, she always came to mind.

Frances had a very wonderful fulfilling life. She had many accomplishments, but most of all she was herself. To me there is no greater gift in life than to be who you are, and do what you want most in life. Every time I come down a mountain, my thoughts of her will be there. But what wonderful thoughts and feelings they will be."

Ellen B. Smith, East Wenatchee, Washington

"Frances was a very special person, not only to her family, but to many, many others. I will always treasure my memories of the many times I spent with her and of our friendship over the years."

Dorothy Jeske Frieske, Spokane, Washington

"I have so many happy memories of growing up with Frances. As I grow older, I seem to treasure these more."

Berniece Werner Smith, Peshastin, Washington

"With her music and her work on the mountain she was probably closer to God than any of us."

Maxie Mae Baker Brooks, Inglewood California

(Maxie was a member of Frances' Camp Fire Girls group. They, along with five other girls, received Torch Bearer Rank, the highest rank, equivalent of Eagle Scout for boys.)

"The year Frances separated from Al, we were at Diamond Head Chalet in Garibaldi Park in Canada. We had with us three grandchildren and our son-in-law, who had just separated from our daughter. (Our daughter had spent Christmas with us and the children and now they were spending this time with their father and us.)

"We had known Frances before and talked to her casually while we were at the chalet, but it was on the way down that she endeared herself to me forever. Bill and our son-in-law were skiing down and I was taking the children down in the snow cat. Frances was riding down too. Our oldest grandson, Whit, who was six at that time, was very disturbed whenever his father and grandfather were out of sight as they skied down. My heart ached for this little boy who had been so saddened and confus-

131

ed by his parent's separation. I realized that he was afraid that his father might disappear from his life. But I had my hands full with his little brother and cousin.

"Frances seemed to sense the situation. She quietly and kindly turned her full attention on Whit, talking to him, showing him things, reassuring him and steadying him all the way down. I was profoundly grateful.

"About eight years later she met Whit again while we were at Adventure Chalet. Neither she nor Whit remembered their previous encounter, but once again she made a positive contribution to his life. Frances had come with Betty Ritter to practice before they performed at Rotary. Somehow she discovered that Whit had his cello there, and before they left she had him playing with her. It was again a lovely, generous act towards a shy child. Later he was to join a youth symphony and I wonder how much this kind of encouragement helped him to get there.

"We didn't see Frances often. We had known of her climbing and admired her even before we met her. It is not only her courage, but even more her kindness that stays with me, and is an everlasting tribute."

Peg and Bill Stark, Leavenworth, Washington

"It was several years after I became a neighbor of her family that I finally met Frances. I knew that she was a very special person from all the reports I'd received, but I didn't realize how unique she really was.

"She had just returned from her first expedition with her husband, Al Randall, and they were visiting her family. I can still see her face as she saw me for the first time with my husband whom she'd known since they were both children. She was wearing jeans and a black "sweat" shirt and her blond hair was bright as copper. Her smile was immediate and lit up her face with radiance. Frances smiled a lot and I felt as if I'd known her all my life from the very beginning of our friendship.

"Perhaps one of the things that we miss most about Frances is the way she made all of us feel better. My son Matt has made the same remark to me when we talk of her. She had a rare quality for making everyone feel important and pertinent, and she was never negative—it just wasn't her style.

"I wish I could have been around her much more than was

possible. It still seems to me that we had so many common interests. Certainly her lifestyle had a quality of self-discipline and interest that was exciting for me to hear about even though she was modest about most of her endeavors. She lived her life to the ultimate measure. She established her own goals and set of values and did not compromise them for the sake of mediocrity. That's truly remarkable for anyone to achieve, regardless of any time frame.

"Frances was the kind of friend that one could always learn from. Her death came too soon.

Shirley McCoy, Peshastin, Washington.

"ON THE MOUNTAIN"

"You ask me
Why do I live on this green mountain?
I smile,
No answer
My heart serene
On flowing water.
Peachblow quietly going
Far away.
This is another earth,
Another sky.
No likeness
To that human world below."

Li Po, 699-762 A.D.,
Chinese Poet of T'ang dynasty

"My cousin, Frances, took treasures with her to the Mountain—Music. A superb violinist, she loved best the music of the winds on the Mountain.

"Music was an affectionate bond between Frances and her Aunt Helen (my mother), a lifelong singer and voice teacher. "Other treasures Frances took to the Mountain—courage, the ability to communicate in many languages she had studied, in order to comfort and save other lives. "City memories Frances

133

shared with us California cousins—Jean, Bud and myself—trips to museums and concerts.

"Country memories we all shared — Lake Wenatchee, watching apples grow and rivers being rafted.

"We talked about Eskimos and American Indians. She knew so much about their languages, art and history. This she shared with us and my husband, Steve, a film artist and historian.

"Frances' soft, shy, unique voice would call us from Alaska, Washington, Mexico, wherever. We looked forward to seeing our beautiful pioneer cousin when she whizzed through L.A., and to hearing the latest thoughts of that brilliant, scientific, mystic, humorous, yet common sense mind.

"Frances and I spoke most of all of family, of her mother, father and brother. She took them and all of us she cared about (including the Crider cousins, Catherine and Cecelia) with her up to her camp on the Mountain. As long as we live, those of us that knew her will be with her, part of us, the part of us that loved her, with her on the Mountain."

Cathleen Potter, Los Angeles, California

The following is a letter by Gordon B. Wright, Professor of Music, University of Alaska, Fairbanks, and Music Director, Fairbanks Symphony Orchestra:

"I first met Frances in 1969 when she joined the violin section of the Fairbanks Symphony and the Arctic Chamber Orchestra. It did not take long to discover that Frances was a multifaceted person with many varied interests, including languages, computers, science and communications.

"It was also evident that she had two overriding passions in her life: music and mountains. Her life in the mountains I only know from reading the newspapers (she had become quite a celebrity on the glacier with her violin), her occasional mountain stories and reports from her friends and acquaintances in the mountain world which has also been an important part of my own life in Alaska.

"She was extremely modest about her musical abilities but during lessons she would often display an amazing technical ability which showed excellent musical training in her early years. She played her violin for any occasion: symphony, chamber music, musicals, opera, dinner music and many church performances. She taught numerous young violinists, most of them eventual members of the orchestra.

"Her thoughtfulness and generosity to her close friends and to the members of the musical community in Fairbanks, her devotion to the Fairbanks Symphony Orchestra enriched all of our lives. Her love of nature and profound concern for the health of the earth's ecosystems were reflected in her lifestyle and professional interests.

"She was one who gave more to the earth than she took."

Gordon B. Wright

Among Frances' papers I found an old envelope with the following written on the back: "From the Northwest Indian News, a memorial addressed to Bernie Whitebear and family over the death of their mother, May Hall Wong—Colville Indian Elder—killed in a traffic accident on Memorial Day:

"Do not stand at my grave and weep,
I am not there. I do not sleep.
I am a thousand winds that blow,
I am the diamond on the snow.
I am the sunlight on the ripened grain,
I am the gentle autumn rain.
When you wake in the morning hush,
I am the swift updrifting rush
Of quiet birds in circling flight,
I'm the soft starlight at night.
Do not stand by my grave and weep."

Author Unknown.

135

Frances gives impromptu open air concert for appreciative climbers.